BATTERSEA

HERE FOR EVERY DOG AND CAT

CAT

PUZZLE BOOK

BATTERSEA

HERE FOR EVERY DOG AND CAT

CAT

PUZZLE BOOK

MORE THAN 100 CAT CONUNDRUMS

WELBECK

Published in 2022 by Welbeck
An Imprint of Welbeck Non-Fiction Limited,
part of Welbeck Publishing Group.
Based in London and Sydney.
www.welbeckpublishing.com

Produced under license from Battersea Dogs Home Ltd to go towards
supporting the work of Battersea Dogs & Cats Home (registered
charity no 206394). For all licensed products sold by Welbeck across
their Battersea range, Welbeck will donate a minimum of £10,000
plus VAT in royalties to Battersea Dogs Home Limited, which gives all
its profits to Battersea Dogs & Cats Home. Battersea.org.uk

All puzzles created by The Puzzle House except Multiple Chews,
created by Ian Greensill.

A CIP catalogue record for this book is available from the
British Library.

ISBN 978 1 80279 413 7

Printed in the UK.

10 9 8 7 6 5 4 3 2 1

SUPPORTING THE WORK OF BATTERSEA

HERE
FOR EVERY
DOG & CAT

Battersea is here for every dog and cat, and has been since 1860.

Battersea takes dogs and cats in, gives them the expert care they need and finds them new homes that are just right for them.

They help pet owners make informed choices, provide training advice, and campaign for changes in the law.

And they help other rescue centres and charities at home and abroad because they want to be here for every dog and cat, wherever they are, for as long as they need Battersea.

Your purchase will help Battersea continue its important work.

Thank you.

battersea.org.uk

Contents

PUZZLES

KEEP IN SHAPE

Solution on page 225.

Individual letters have been replaced by symbols. The first group stands for the letters T, R, A and Y – making the word TRAY.

The symbols remain constant throughout all the groups. What cat-related words do the other groups make?

A TO Z

Solution on page 225.

Here's an A to Z of cat-related words (minus an X!). The words are hidden in the letter square. All words are in straight lines and can go horizontally, vertically and diagonally. They may read forwards or backwards.

There are two words that appear twice. Can you track them down?

ADORABLE	JUMP	SEARCH
BOLD	KITTEN	TWITCH
CUNNING	LAZY	UPKEEP
DIGNIFIED	MISCHIEVOUS	VENTURE
ELEGANT	NIMBLE	WALK
FAMILIAR	OBSERVE	YOUNG
GUARDED	POUNCE	ZEAL
HANDSOME	QUICKLY	
INDEPENDENT	REMARKABLE	

```
D  V  Y  T  N  E  D  N  E  P  E  D  N  I  F
I  L  A  E  R  Z  D  U  G  T  J  Q  U  A  Z
G  H  E  D  T  L  R  V  N  A  W  U  M  Y  E
N  E  S  U  O  V  E  I  H  C  S  I  M  H  O
I  R  D  B  L  R  M  L  W  A  L  K  T  P  R
F  Z  D  A  E  B  A  E  P  I  N  T  O  C  D
I  J  E  R  L  U  R  B  A  X  N  B  R  E  H
E  Z  H  E  S  U  K  R  L  A  S  W  D  W  H
D  G  A  C  T  O  A  T  G  E  P  R  E  N  A
I  N  N  N  R  M  B  E  R  P  A  C  E  Y  N
Q  U  E  I  L  A  L  V  E  U  O  T  O  Z  D
A  V  O  T  N  E  E  U  G  Y  T  U  M  A  S
B  L  E  G  T  N  O  S  Y  I  N  Q  N  L  O
R  Y  L  K  C  I  U  Q  K  G  E  B  E  C  M
U  P  K  E  E  P  K  C  T  N  A  G  E  L  E
```

FITTING IN

Solution on page 226.

We all hope that a newcomer to the home will fit in as one of the family. In this puzzle a word with a feline feel about it has to be fitted into the spaces so that the word becomes complete.

All the words in 1 need the same three-letter word, and a similar pattern follows for 2 and 3. Three different words for three different sections.

1. _ _ _ A T O

   A _ _ _ I S E R

   S _ _ _ A C H

2. S _ _ _ S T I C K

   C O L _ _ _ S E

   O V E R _ _ _

3. _ _ _ K I N

   S _ _ _ S H O T

   C A _ _ _ E S

CAT BASKET

Solution on page 226.

The cats need to go in their basket. In the letter box the word CATS appears along with three other words of four letters. The words appear in straight lines of letters that can go across, back, up, down or diagonally.

Use these words to fill the empty basket by creating a word square in which the words read the same going across and down.

A	R	E	A	L	Q
W	S	W	J	W	U
E	A	A	S	X	W
Y	L	T	M	W	O
Z	A	Y	R	E	W
C	Z	T	E	A	M

QUIZ CROSSWORD

Solution on page 227.

Solve the answer to each question in order to complete the grid.

ACROSS

3. Arguably cats' most important senses are in which part of their bodies? (5)
7. What is another name for character or personality? (6)
8. Which word can mean out of sorts, maybe like a shellfish? (6)
10. London's White City was home to a record breaker in what rodent-chasing role? (3.7)
11. What is another word for gentle, or a genre? (4)
12. What means a typical cat cry was made? (5)
13. What does a cat need in addition to care? (9)
16. What is a movie, feline or otherwise, screened during the day called? (7)
21. Which science is used to discover family trees in the animal and human world? (9)
22. Which important sense does not include sight or sound? (5)
23 **& 9 Down.** Which former Lord Mayor of London famously had a cat? (4)
24. What describes a cat who looks good in pictures taken by a camera? (10)
26. What might a mouse's emotion be when faced with a cat? (6)
27. What is another word for indigenous? (6)
28. In the past cats have been hard at work on which sea-going vessels? (5)

DOWN

1. Which cat colour shares its name with a toffee? (7)
2. Which parts of a cat's anatomy are concerned with movement? (7)
3. Which measure that goes with inches is another name for paws? (4)
4. What might be left on the skin if a cat has been in a fight? (4)
5. Which containers are used to transport animals to the cattery or vet? (7)
6. What word means to leave behind or forsake? (7)
9. See 23 Across. (11)
14. What follows 'cats' in the name of road markings? (4)
15. What does a Manx cat not have? (4)
17. What might a sorceress's cat do to enchant or captivate? (7)
18. Which name of a Scottish town and an adventurer precedes Rex in a breed of cat? (7)
19. Which ribbon is awarded at a cat show? (7)
20. Which word for accomplish might be rewarded with 19 Down? (7)
24. What can be found on the underside of 3 Down? (4)
25. What is another word for possesses, whether it's a cat or a place where they stay? (4)

STRAY CAT

Solution on page 227.

The three letters in the word CAT have been replaced by question marks in the word below. Each question mark could be an A, a C or a T. It could be only one, two or three of those letters, or it could be more than one of any as well.

The other letters of the alphabet are in place. Can you replace the question marks with C, A or T to find the word?

We give you a clue to help you see that the stray cat makes it home.

? ? ? ? S ? R O P H I ?

CLUE:
Disastrous

NINE LIVES

Solution on page 228.

Nine boxes. Nine different letters of the alphabet. Solve the cunning clues and write the letters in the appropriate spaces in the grid.

When all nine letters are in place the first name of a feline character from poetry is created.

CLUES

1. Pictures taken with a camera   6 7 5 4 5 3

2. They are used for biting and chewing   4 8 8 4 7

3. Grooms with a tool which contains bristles
    1 9 2 3 7 8 3

1	2	3	4	5	6	7	8	9

CLOCK WATCH

Solution on page 228.

In this puzzle each answer has eight letters. Write the answer words in the grid, with each first letter going in a numbered square. Then you have to decide whether to write the answer in a clockwise or anti-clockwise direction. All the answers have to interlock together.

CLUES

1. Upholstered seat, ideal cat comfort

2. Connoisseurs of the cat world

3. Tame, homely

4. Breed which resembles long-haired Siamese

5. Looked for a cat which was missing

6. Gave a treat for a deed well done

7. Predecessor, it might have come from Africa, America or India

8. Picked or chose a favourite feline

CAT NAP

Solution on page 228.

Coco, Milo, Molly, Poppy and Rosie are five felines who all live at the same house. They are all inside enjoying a nap. One cat has been asleep for 20 minutes, one for 30 minutes, one for 40 minutes, one for 70 minutes and one for 80 minutes.

The cats are snoozing in different parts of the house. The dining room, the hall, the kitchen, the landing and the lounge are the places where the cats have found their own space. From the clues can you work out where each cat is and how long they have been taking a nap?

The combined time that Poppy and Rosie have been napping comes to the same amount of minutes that the cat in the lounge has been sleeping.

Coco is not the cat who has slept for exactly 20 minutes in the kitchen.

Milo has been napping twice as long as the cat in the dining room.

Molly napped ten minutes less than the cat on the landing who wasn't Rosie.

SHADY SEVENS

Solution on page 228.

Place all the listed seven-letter words to read across the grid in such an order that the diagonal line of letters in the shaded seven spaces forms the name of a breed of cat.

BASKETS

CLIMBED

FASTEST

NIBBLES

PLAYFUL

POSTURE

STRIPED

SIX FIX

Solution on page 229.

All answers have six letters and fit into the grid reading in a clockwise direction. We give you the starting point for the answer to Clue 1, but after that you have to work out in which hexagonal cell the answer begins.

CLUES

1. Relating to cats

2. Eating

3. Hey diddle diddle, the cat and the _____

4. Choose, pick

5. Jewelled headdresses to dress up your cat

6. Express approval

7. Rely on

8. Hug, embrace

9. Bend down, as a cat does before pouncing

10. Shape of a show ring

11. Gambol, play

12. Search for food in the wild

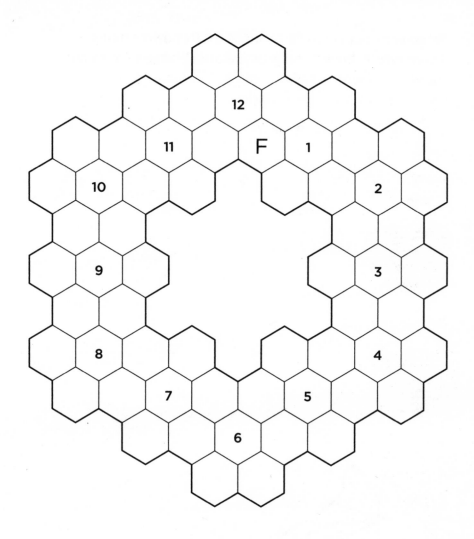

THAT'S MY CAT

Solution on page 229.

There is no doubting the breed of cat this owner has.
Rearrange all the letters in the personal name to form the
name of the type of cat.

S I A N   N A I S B Y

CLUE:
One word

ALPHAGRAMS

Solution on page 229.

Cats can appear on stage and screen. The titles of cat-friendly films and pantomimes have had the letters in their names mixed up and rearranged in alphabetical order.

Can you work them all out? We give you the number of words in the title.

1. A A C F H I N N O O O O R T T T
   (six words)

2. A A B C L L O T U
   (two words)

3. A A C E H N P S S S T T U W W Y ?
   (three words)

4. B I N O O P S S S T U
   (three words)

5. A A C C D D G H H I I I I K N N N
   O S T T T T W
   (five words)

CATWALK

Solution on page 230.

A straightforward crossword to stroll through.

ACROSS

8. Teach, especially how to care for a cat (7)
9. Soil (5)
10. Supple, agile (5)
11. Saviour, liberator from danger (7)
12. Hard areas on the underside of the paw (4)
13. Abroad, where many breeds hail from (8)
16. The state of being fully grown (8)
18. Festival, celebration (4)
21. Part of the day before the favoured time of a nocturnal animal (7)
23. Cat's cry (5)
25. Escape, dodge (5)
26. Female parents (7)

DOWN

1. Tinkling collar accessory (4)
2. Pursued prey (6)
3. Tapped with the foot (5)
4. Bring up, raise (4)
5. Non-working time (7)
6. Wake up from a sleep (6)
7. Fascination, great charm (8)
12. Spoiled, over-indulged (8)
14. Animal clinician (3)
15. Tracked (7)
17. Dr Seuss story, *The Cat in* _____ _____ (3.3)
19. Astounded by an achievement or feat (6)
20. Hit hard (5)
22. Play activity (4)
24. Clean with water (4)

FELINE FIVES

Solution on page 230.

Solve the cat-based clues, which are listed at random.

Each five-letter answer starts in a space with an odd number (1, 3, 5, 7, 9 and 11) and ends in a space with an even number (2, 4, 6, 8, 10 and 12).

The letter in space 1 is M.

CLUES

Mature cat

A cat's rate of this is much faster than a human's

This word for a passage precedes 'cat' to describe a feral feline

Things to eat

Characteristic

Cat sound

REHOMING

Solution on page 231.

Here's a list of words that are all connected with rehoming cats. Find the correct home for all the words by fitting them in place in the grid to read either across or down.

There is only one way to fit all the words back.

3 LETTERS

OWN

PET

VET

4 LETTERS

CARE

CHAT

HELP

HOME

SUIT

5 LETTERS

ADOPT

FORMS

MATCH

NEEDS

6 LETTERS

ADVICE

CHANCE

DETAIL

RESCUE

SEARCH

UNIQUE

7 LETTERS

ADDRESS

SUPPORT

8 LETTERS

GUIDANCE

REGISTER

SUITABLE

9 LETTERS

BEHAVIOUR

EMOTIONAL

MICROCHIP

QUESTIONS

REWARDING

10 LETTERS

CHARACTERS

EXPERIENCE

INDIVIDUAL

11 LETTERS

PREFERENCES

TEMPERAMENT

12 LETTERS

VACCINATIONS

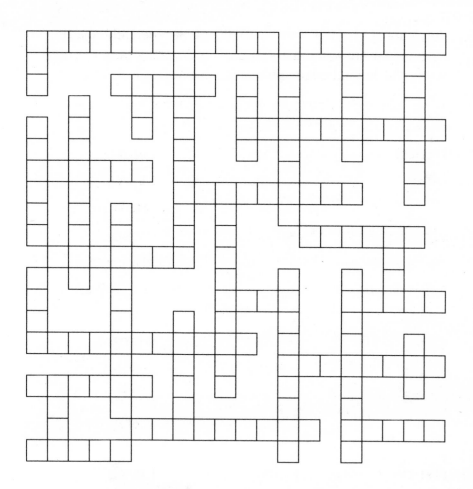

CAT COLLAR

Solution on page 231.

Solve the clues, which are in no particular order, and slot the seven-letter answers back into their correct places in the cat collar. The last letter of one answer is also the first letter of the next.

Answer 1 begins with a letter C.

CLUES

Looking like a cherub, totally innocent

Place to send your pet when you are on holiday

Refuse receptacle where a scavenger might hunt

There is evidence cats may have lived in Cyprus 8,000 years ago. What is this country's divided capital?

Longed for, pined

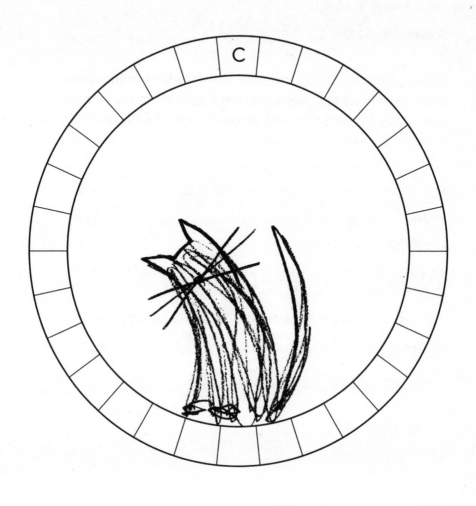

HIDE AND SEEK

Solution on page 232.

In this puzzle you must seek out the names of artists and painters who have included cats in their works. The names are hidden in the sentences below and can be found by linking words or parts of words together.

1. Parliament Hill cat colony, in Ottawa in Canada, closed in 2013

2. I found my cat Tom an eternal problem, always trying to escape

3. Chase the cat and climb that tree for a dare? No, I really meant it

4. A lecture on cats is a wonderful topic as sometimes happens

5. Some time ago yards of wool were unravelled by the kittens

PET'S GARDEN

Solution on page 232.

Can you fill the empty spaces with only the letters C, A or T to name some things found in a feline-friendly garden?

1. _ _ _ M I N _
   (herb)

2. _ _ _ _ I _
   (tree)

3. _ _ R N _ _ I O N
   (flower)

4. _ H R Y S _ N _ H E M U M
   (flower)

5. N I _ O _ I N _
   (flower)

6. _ E R R _ _ O _ _ _ P O _ S
   (plant holders)

GIVE ME FIVE!

Solution on page 232.

Solve the clues, which are listed at random. All the answers contain five letters. You have to fit the answers back in the frame, going either across or down.

There is a starter letter to help you on the way. There is only one way to fit all the words back.

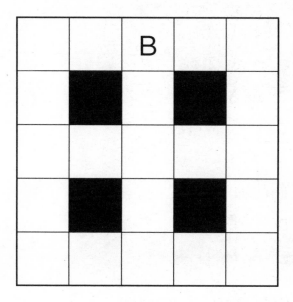

CLUES

Units of time to measure a cat's age

Enticing smell of food being prepared

All cats have this circulating through their bodies

Train or instruct your cat

Remains out of view while weighing up a situation

Type of cat mottled with dark stripes

CAT'S CRADLE

Solution on page 233.

The letters in SEVEN words to actions a cat might make have been rearranged in alphabetical order. Can you put the letters back in their correct order and slot them in the grid?

When you have done so, the centre column reading down will spell out the name of a breed of cat, and the horizontal 4 across will reveal the name of an island that is its near neighbour.

1. A C E M P R S

2. A B D E E H V

3. A B G I L M N

4. A A M R S T U

5. A G I L N P Y

6. A C D E E P S

7. A D E E M N R

1						
2						
3						
4						
5						
6						
7						

MULTIPLE CHEWS

Solution on page 233.

Chew on these multiple-choice quiz questions, based on well-known television cats.

1. In the 1970s sitcom *Rising Damp*, what was the name of Rigsby's cat?

   A Copenhagen

   B Lisbon

   C Paris

   D Vienna

2. The cat-like Meowth featured in which animated TV series?

   A *Dinosaur King*

   B *Dragon Drive*

   B *Monster Rancher*

   D *Pokémon*

3. Lord Tubbington and Mr Puss are cats who appeared in which US TV series?

   A *90210*

   B *Fame*

   C *Glee*

   D *High School Musical*

4. In *Star Trek: The Next Generation*, the ginger cat Spot belongs to which character?

A Data

B Deanna Troi

C Geordi La Forge

D Worf

5. In *The Big Bang Theory*, Sheldon Cooper names all of his 25 cats after Manhattan Project scientists apart from which one?

A Dazzles

B Frazzles

C Snazzles

D Zazzles

6. A cat called Ser Pounce appeared in which TV series?

A *Britannia*

B *Game of Thrones*

C *His Dark Materials*

D *Westworld*

7. The TV series *8 Out of 10 Cats* first aired in 2005, but where did the name originate?

A Advertising slogan

B Film quote

C Novel

D Pop group

8. What was the name of the eponymous stuffed cat who comes to life in the animated children's TV series?

A Bagpuss

B Bigpuss

C Ragpuss

D Snagpuss

9. In *Sabrina the Teenage Witch*, Sabrina's cat had the same name as which American state capital?

A Jackson

B Lincoln

C Salem

D Trenton

10. *C.A.T.S. Eyes*, a police drama that ran from 1985 to 1987 starring Jill Gascoine, was a spin-off of which earlier police drama?

A *Juliet Bravo*

B *Softly, Softly*

C *The Gentle Touch*

D *The Sweeney*

11. In *Red Dwarf*, what was the rather unimaginative name of the cat character played by Danny John-Jules?

A Cat

B Kit

C Moggy

D Puss

12. In *Friends*, which character wrote a song (which turned into a jingle) called 'Smelly Cat'?

A Monica

B Phoebe

C Rachel

D Ross

MYSTIC MOG

Solution on page 234.

If you want to foresee the unseen, then send for Mystic Mog, the cat who knows it's not what you see that matters ... it's what you cannot see! There's a jumble of letters of the alphabet in the box.

What you need to find are the letters that do not appear. Use each missing letter once only to make the name of something that most cats like to drink.

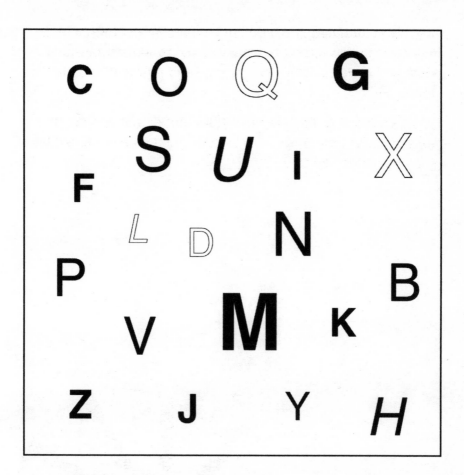

THAT'S MY CAT

Solution on page 234.

There is no doubting the breed of cat this owner has.
Rearrange all the letters in the personal name to form the
name of the type of cat.

L I S A   J A N E   P O B B E A T

CLUE:

Two words

SPLITS

Solution on page 234.

The names of colours of cats have been divided into a line of letters. Can you work out the names of the two colours in each case?

1 is two colours of four letters, 2 is two colours of five letters, and in 3 there are two six-letter colours. The letters read in chronological order.

1. B S E L U A E L

2. B C L R A E A C M K

3. B S I R O L V N E Z E R

SIX FIX

Solution on page 235.

All answers have six letters and fit into the grid reading in a clockwise direction. We give you the starting point for the answer to Clue 1, but after that you have to work out in which hexagonal cell the answer begins.

CLUES

1. Breed of cat with long hair originating in Turkiye

2. Correct, suitable

3. Express a liking for one breed over another

4. Distinguish one category in a cat show

5. Commands, instructs

6. Pamper, over-indulge

7. Lively, always on the move

8. Give time unreservedly

9. One who patrols a designated area

10. Nibbled, ate something hard with small bites

11. Tapping or dabbing with the foot

12. Arouse from sleep

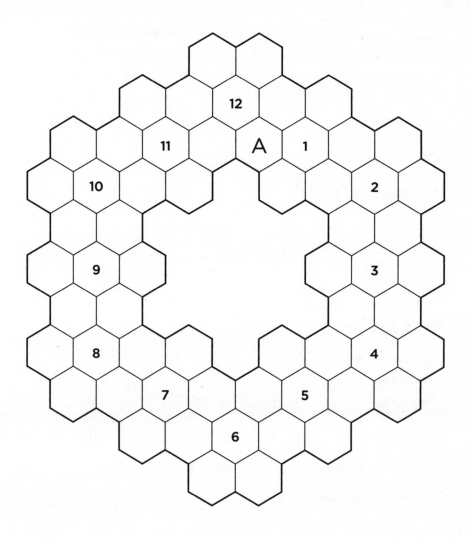

WHO AM I?

Solution on page 235.

Use the clues in the rhyme to find the letters to name
a famous feline.

Use all the clues and spell out my name.

My first is in FOE
And also in FRIEND

My second is in BREAK
And also in MEND

My third is in LISTEN
And also in CALL

My fourth is in TAIL
But isn't in TALL

My fifth is in MIX
But isn't in FAME

SEALPOINT

Solution on page 235.

Each answer contains FOUR letters. The first letter goes in a numbered triangle, the second letter directly above it, the third letter to the right and the fourth to the left. Answer words interlock in the completed pointed grid.

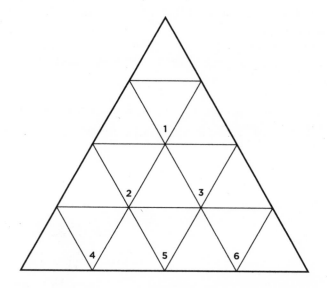

CLUES

1. Shout a cat's name to bring it back

2. Run away, especially when faced with a problem

3. Cat colour, the same as a clear sky

4. Domestic animals in general

5. Owned and looked after a cat

6. Leap, bound

KEPT SAFE

Solution on page 236.

Each of the 26 letters of the alphabet has been replaced by a number from 1 to 26. Work out which number represents which letter to complete the crossword-style grid, which has words reading across and down. You are given the letters in the word KEPT to start you off. 1 = K, 2 = E, 3 = P, 4 = T. Straight away you can fill in all the squares that contain the numbers 1, 2, 3 and 4.

Fill in the 1 to 26 grid with letters of the alphabet as you work them out.

When you have worked out the code, the letters 15, 11, 24, 16, 15, 11, 24, 19, 19, 5, 9 will spell out a breed of cat.

15	11	24	16	15	11	24	19	19	5	9

Codeword grid (numbers 1–26):

C1	C2	C3	C4	C5	C6	C7	C8	C9	C10	C11	C12	C13	C14	C15
	15		19		21				19		8		15	
15	6	8	24	7	6	9		16	5	17	2	4	5	14
	4		4		24		15		12		9		19	
1	2	3	4		15	11	5	9	2		4	5	24	19
			2		1		17				24		15	
5	19	2	8	4		15	7	17	3	5	16	24	7	16
	24		9		26		6		24		10			
8	2	25		3	2	8	20	2	15	4		14	2	26
			9		5		19		1		23		5	
16	7	15	4	6	8	16	5	19		3	6	8	8	9
	15		8				10		9		17			
19	24	22	2		9	15	2	16	4		3	2	4	9
	15		4		2		26		8		24		24	
13	5	4	15	11	2	9		18	5	13	16	24	16	10
	4		11		1			18			10		18	

Solution key:

1	2	3	4	5	6	7	8	9	10	11	12	13

14	15	16	17	18	19	20	21	22	23	24	25	26

SHADOW PLAY

Solution on page 236.

Answer the questions going across in the top grid. All answers have seven letters. When the top grid is complete, take the letters in the shaded squares and place them vertically, one below the other, in the lower grid.

When you have completed the lower grid, a famous expression with a feline connection will be revealed.

CLUES

1. The very noisiest in a group of cats

2. Extremely old, such as times in Egypt when cats were much revered

3. Male felines

4. Leap from the ground ready to pounce (4.3)

5. Possess characteristics from previous generations

6. Not usually a pet, but a very speedy member of the cat family

7. Test to make sure a cat is in good health (5.2)

8. Striped pet cats

9. Attaching some form of identity as a tracking measure

10. Presenting a cat in a particular display or exhibition

1	▓		▓				
2					▓		▓
3	▓	▓					
4	▓						▓
4			▓				▓
6				▓			▓
7	▓		▓				
8		▓	▓				
9	▓	▓					
10			▓				▓

Z
Z
z

1	2	3	4	5	6	7	8	9	10

TAGS

Solution on page 236.

The letters on the cat tags can be rearranged to form words. There are letters on individual tags, shared letters between two tags, and the space in the middle needs to be filled by a letter that is in all three tags.

You are looking for the names of three different cat colours.

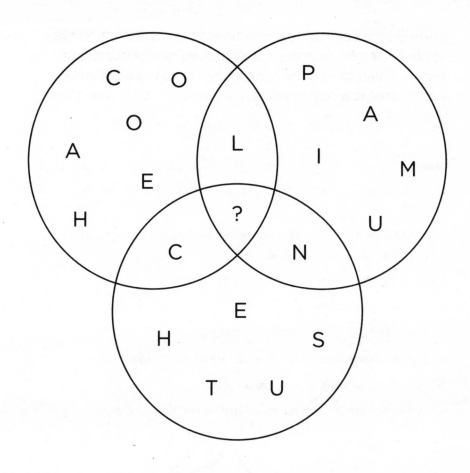

CLOCK WATCH

Solution on page 237.

In this puzzle each answer has eight letters. Write the answer words in the grid, with each first letter going in a numbered square. Then you have to decide whether to write the answer in a clockwise or anti-clockwise direction. All the answers have to interlock together.

CLUES

1. Special feline events, the first was in the Crystal Palace in 1871 (3.5)

2. Biblical boat, where the Manx cat reputedly lost its tail trapping it in a door (5.3)

3. Goes back to a previous haunt or territory

4. Roamed, rambled

5. Coat which is thick, hard and springy

6. The formal acceptance of a stray cat to its new home

7. The spine, a cat's is very strong

8. In a UK town it's a pavement but in the USA it's a _____

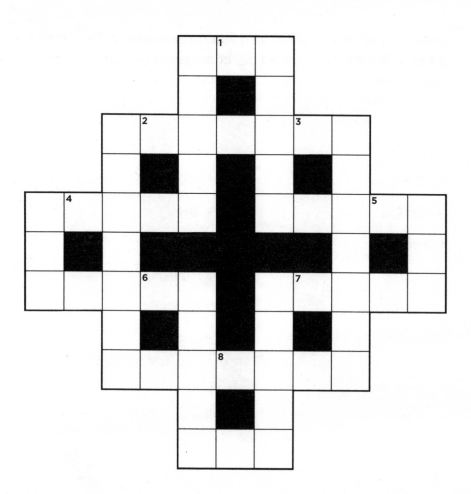

ALL THE SEVENS

Solution on page 237.

The listed cat-linked words all contain seven letters. Fit them all back in the frame to read either across or down. One letter is keyed in.

Take care! There is only one way to get all the words back in place.

ADDRESS

BASKETS

BLINKED

DIETARY

ESSENCE

FRIENDS

INSPECT

KITTENS

PURRING

SNOOZED

STATELY

SUN TRAP

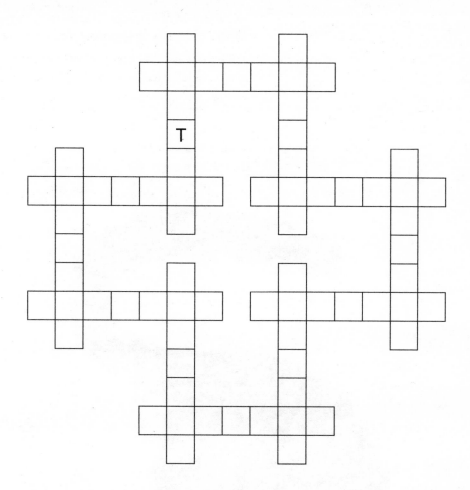

NUMBER NAMES

Solution on page 238.

What's a cat worth? They are all beyond price, of course. However, with these cats we have taken the letters from their names and given them each a value.

Six different letters in all are used. The numbers allocated are between 1 and 6. The total of each name is worked out by adding individual letters together.

M I A = 6

M I L O = 1 3

M I L L Y = 1 6

M O L L Y = 2 1

What is L O L A worth?

CAT CODES

Solution on page 238.

Answer the questions across in the upper grid. All answers have eight letters. Take the key-coded letters and place them in the lower grid. For example, the first letter you need is an A in square C1.

When you have finished, a proverb with a feline connection will be revealed.

CLUES

1. A cat which has won a number of shows

2. Shorthair breed, similar to the Siamese

3. Patterns on a cat's fur

4. English queen who popularised the Persian breed in the 19th century

5. People use a cattery for their pets when they take these

6. Facial hairs

7. Pedigree, upbringing

8. A grey colour, not to be confused with barbecue fuel!

9. A colour, which shares its name with a precious metal

10. The seasonal shedding of hair

	A	B	C	D	E	F	G	H
1								
2								
3								
4								
5								
6								
7								
8								
9								
10								

C1	H2	C5		C4	G8	D9	H3		B3	B7	D2
H10	D8	F6	G5		F10	F9		D4	B1	D7	
E5	H4	B2	E6								

CATWALK

Solution on page 239.

A straightforward crossword to stroll through.

ACROSS

8. To cause chaos, the proverb says to put the cat _____ the pigeons (7)
9. Decorate, as you might add an accessory to your cat (5)
10. Bones in the head (5)
11. Edge of a roof a fearless feline might jump from (7)
12. Organs of sight (4)
13. A spice, and a cat colour (8)
16. If one cat has nine lives, how many would two cats have? (8)
18. Notice, locate (4)
21. Touch, meet (7)
23. Listened, perceived (5)
25. Gland on the foot pad which leaves a scent (5)
26. Small rodents which might be prey (7)

DOWN

1. Feet (4)
2. The level of noise (6)
3. Lively, graceful (5)
4. Halt, stay (4)
5. Sponsors of charities or fundraising events (7)
6. Fluffy ball as a plaything (6)
7. Feeling, intuition (8)
12. Practice, movement (8)
14. Slippery surface (3)
15. Sly, furtive approach (7)
17. Male or female (6)
19. Calm, unruffled (6)
20. Opposite of long when describing cats' hair (5)
22. All in order (4)
24. Food plan (4)

WITH CAT-LIKE TREAD

Solution on page 240.

All the listed words are about how cats move. The words are hidden in the letter square. All words are in straight lines and can go horizontally, vertically and diagonally. They may read forwards or backwards.

AMBLE	MOVE	SLITHER
BOUND	POUNCE	STALK
CHASE	PROCEED	STEP
CRAWL	PROGRESS	STROLL
CREEP	PROWL	TRACE
FOLLOW	PURSUE	TRACK
HUNT	SAUNTER	TREAD
LEAP	SHADOW	WALK
LURK	SLINK	

S	H	L	L	O	R	T	S	N	P	J	S
T	A	J	U	S	A	R	P	T	E	H	M
R	E	U	L	L	M	E	X	R	A	Y	K
A	S	I	N	I	B	A	C	D	O	L	A
C	N	L	S	T	L	D	O	A	A	W	K
K	I	T	L	H	E	W	N	W	R	G	L
B	E	E	P	E	E	R	C	U	S	T	E
P	A	V	C	R	L	U	R	K	O	T	U
P	R	O	O	N	E	S	A	H	C	B	S
J	R	S	R	M	U	E	W	A	R	I	R
P	T	N	U	H	F	O	L	L	O	W	U
S	S	E	R	G	O	R	P	A	D	E	P

MULTIPLE CHEWS

Solution on page 241.

Chew on these multiple-choice quiz questions, a test of your general feline knowledge.

1. The human skeleton has 206 bones but how many does a cat have?

    A 170

    B 190

    c 210

    D 230

2. Manx cats, which have hardly any tail, hail from which island?

    A Guernsey

    B Isle of Man

    c Isle of Wight

    D Jersey

3. Which ancient people considered cats to be sacred?

    A Aztecs

    B Egyptians

    c Incans

    D Romans

4. *Kattenstoet* (Festival of the Cats) is an annual parade held in which Belgian city?

A Antwerp

B Liège

C Mons

D Ypres

5. What is the nickname of the F-14 US jet fighter?

A Tomcat

B Bobcat

C Wildcat

D Angry cat

6. How many toes does a cat typically have?

A 14

B 16

C 18

D 20

7. Which famous inventor is reputedly thought to have made the first cat flap?

A Albert Einstein

B Isaac Newton

C Michael Faraday

D Thomas Edison

8. One of the largest domestic cat breeds is named after a US state where it originated – which one?

A Maine Coon

B Minnesota Coon

C Mississippi Coon

D Montana Coon

9. How many eyelids does a cat have on each eye?

A 1

B 2

C 3

D 4

10. 'Billy the Cat' was a character first seen in 1967 in which comic?

A *The Beano*

B *The Beezer*

C *The Dandy*

D *The Topper*

11. Creme Puff, from Austin, Texas, is the oldest cat ever recorded. What age did she live to (in years)?

A 34

B 36

C 38

D 40

12. What is the name for a group of cats?

A Caravan

B Cast

C Cete

D Clowder

STRAY CAT

Solution on page 241.

The three letters in the word CAT have been replaced by question marks in the word below. Each question mark could be an A, a C or a T. It could be only one, two or three of those letters, or it could be more than one of any as well.

The other letters of the alphabet are in place. Can you replace the question marks with C, A or T to find the word?

We give you a clue to help you see that the stray cat makes it home.

I N ? ? N ? ? ? I O N

CLUE:
A magic formula or spell

KEEP IN SHAPE

Solution on page 241.

Individual letters have been replaced by symbols. The first group stands for the letters M, O, U, S and E – making the word MOUSE. The symbols remain constant throughout all the groups. What cat-related words do the other groups make?

CRYPTI-CAT

Solution on page 242.

A cat-based crossword with a cryptic twist.

ACROSS

3. Frighten as car exceeds speed limit (5)
6. Cat's feet have a temporary break, we hear (4)
7. Eats messily after loud noise. A fine spread! (5)
8. Get out of bed earning extra wages (4)
10. Quietly in the hay, the cat is content (5)
14. Describes the touch of fur? That's silly! (4)
15. Try to teach a cat in the light rain (5)
16. Picture the sound of a twig breaking (4)
17. Sounds like a path to find out how heavy your pet is (5)

DOWN

1. Games and exercise from developing ports (5)
2. Really smart movement of a cat's tail (5)
4. Slinks along detestable people (6)
5. Look at your estimate for a catnap (4)
9. Feeding a mixture of gin with tea (6)
11. Offspring not old (5)
12. Kitten's first walk around muddled pests (5)
13. Family history climbed by a cat (4)

TAKE A TUMBLE

Solution on page 242.

Cats don't always land unhurt if they take a tumble, but because of their powers of balance and coordination, they often come down to earth safe and sound.

In each of the sentences below, there are three words which are made up of the same letters. They are anagrams of each other. Can you tumble the letters around and work out what they are? Happy landing!

1. We have to cater for a wide variety of diets as some animals react to food in different ways. Cleanliness is paramount so no trace of any contamination is vital.

2. Our cat was rescued by the brave people in the fire brigade. Our garden is now well and truly secured, which reduces the risk of the same thing happening again.

3. My neighbour's pet feline Andrew has been known to wander off away from home for long periods at a time. I have warned her that it might not be safe for him to do so.

NUMBER SUMS

Solution on page 243.

Work out the number sums with a difference below. Cat-linked calculations and mathematical magic combine.

A. The number of tails on three Bobcats multiplied by the number of letters in the name of the girl who met the Cheshire Cat in Wonderland.

B. The number following 19 in the year Tom and Jerry made their debut, plus the number following 19 when Figaro the little black-and-white kitten appeared in the movie *Pinocchio*.

C. Add together the digits in the year in which Walt Disney authorised his final film before his death. The year starts with one and ends in zero.

WHAT'S MY LINE?

Solution on page 243.

Cat lovers have all sorts of jobs and professions. Can you fill the empty spaces with the letters C, A or T to complete the occupations of the feline owners?

1. _ _ _ O R

2. _ E _ _ H E R

3. _ _ _ O U N _ _ N _

4. _ R _ H I _ E _ _

5. _ _ _ U _ R Y

6. _ _ R _ O O N I S _

SEALPOINT

Solution on page 243.

Each answer contains FOUR letters. The first letter goes in a numbered triangle, the second letter directly above it, the third letter to the right and the fourth to the left. Answer words interlock in the completed pointed grid.

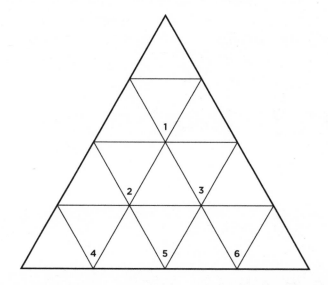

CLUES

1. Eat a main meal

2. Animal clinicians

3. Twist or tangle in a ball of wool used as a toy

4. Catch sight of when prowling

5. Pace, stride

6. Change position

FITTING IN

Solution on page 243.

We all hope that a newcomer to the home will fit in as one of the family. In this puzzle, a word with a feline feel about it has to be fitted in to the spaces so that the word becomes complete.

All the words in 1 need the same three-letter word, 2 and 3 need a different four-letter word. Three different words for three different sections.

1. A L _ _ _ S

   B E _ _ _ V E D

   C O L _ _ _ R Y

2. M O _ _ _ _

   C _ _ _ _ M A N

   A R M C _ _ _ _

3. H _ _ _ _ A Y

   F O R E B _ _ _ _

   G _ _ _ _ T I C K

FELIDAE CLOSE

Solution on page 244.

There are six properties in Felidae Close, with a different cat living at each house. From the clues can you work out where each cat lives?

CLUES

Flo's house has an even number

Snowy has a neighbouring cat on either side and both have names starting with a letter in the second half of the alphabet

Lily lives at number 2 Felidae Close

Tom lives in a house with a higher number than the houses of both Milo and Tigger

NINE LIVES

Solution on page 244.

Nine boxes. Nine different letters of the alphabet. Solve the cunning clues and write the letters in the appropriate spaces in the grid.

When all nine letters are in place, the name for the short, soft hairs at the base of the cat's fur is created.

CLUES

1. Spherical like a ball to play with   5 7 1 2 3

2. Special reward   9 5 4 8 9

3. Animated entertainment such as the classic *Tom and Jerry*
   6 8 5 9 7 7 2

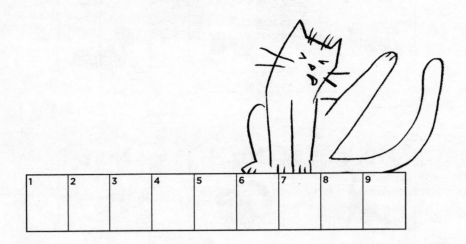

1	2	3	4	5	6	7	8	9

GIVE ME FIVE!

Solution on page 245.

Solve the clues, which are listed at random. All the answers contain five letters. You have to fit the answers back in the frame, going either across or down.

There is a starter letter to help you on the way. There is only one way to fit all the words back.

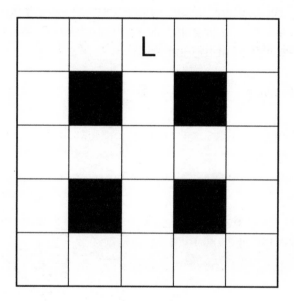

CLUES

Short-haired cat breed the Havana _____

Parts of the skin which are tender or broken

All animals use these to pick up scent

Movie award and a very popular cat name

This word goes after 'Cat' in a popular Lakeland walk near Keswick

Gently passes the tongue over when washing and preening

FOOD FOR THOUGHT

Solution on page 245.

Five cats have different owners. Each cat has a different coat colour and has a different favourite food. From the clues given can you match the owners to their cats, and decide on the coat colouring and favourite dish?

When you discover a positive piece of information that definitely links things together, put a tick in the appropriate space in the grid. Put a cross in any space where you are sure there cannot be a link. Keep re-reading the clues and adding ticks or crosses until you can work out the full solution.

CLUES

1. Mr Martin has a white cat who likes chicken

2. The tabby cat who likes sardines is not called Lucy

3. Ms Neale's cat Daisy likes liver, but Ms Lucas's cat does not like tuna

4. Mr Jones owns neither the ginger cat named Jerry, nor the black cat that likes kippers

5. Chloe belongs to one of the ladies

		NAME					FOOD					CAT COLOUR				
		CHLOE	DAISY	FLUFFY	JERRY	LUCY	CHICKEN	KIPPERS	LIVER	SARDINES	TUNA	BLACK	GINGER	GREY	TABBY	WHITE
OWNER	MR JONES															
	MS KENT															
	MS LUCAS															
	MR MARTIN															
	MS NEALE															
CAT COLOUR	BLACK															
	GINGER															
	GREY															
	TABBY															
	WHITE															
FOOD	CHICKEN															
	KIPPERS															
	LIVER															
	SARDINES															
	TUNA															

CAT'S CRADLE

Solution on page 245.

The letters in SEVEN words with a feline link have been rearranged in alphabetical order. Can you put the letters back in their correct order and slot them in the grid?

When you have done so, the centre column reading down will spell out the real name of the cat in the film *Breakfast at Tiffany's,* who in the film was called simply Cat. The horizontal 4 across will reveal the surname of the man who became US President the year the film was released.

1. D E G M O O R

2. A E G H I N R

3. A E H L S T T

4. D E E K N N Y

5. E G G I N R Y

6. E E E K L R S

7. A F L L P U Y

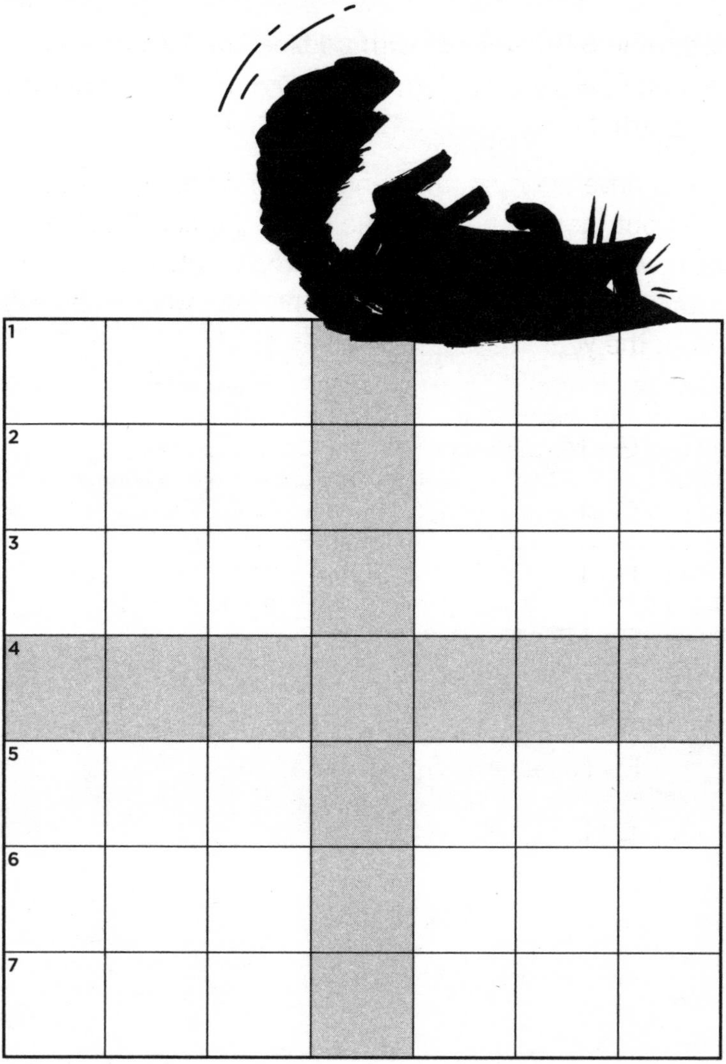
1
2
3
4
5
6
7

CATWALK

Solution on page 246.

A straightforward crossword to stroll through.

ACROSS

8. The opposite of smoother with regard to a cat's coat (7)
9. Spare, reserve (5)
10. Sag in a bedraggled way (5)
11. Stretchy thread on a cat's toy (7)
12. Secure, out of danger (4)
13. A breed of cat from across the Atlantic (8)
16. The study of characteristics from one generation to another (8)
18. Possesses, in charge of (4)
21. Description of a relative who is not close (7)
23. Repeated behaviour (5)
25. Cat colour, or a mauve shade (5)
26. They aid movement in an animal's body (7)

DOWN

1. Reared (4)
2. Escape, flee (3.3)
3. Figure, outline (5)
4. At liberty (4)
5. Mends (7)
6. Not moving, totally still (6)
7. They provide protection against disease (8)
12. Programme for a cat show (8)
14. Came together (3)
15. Go forward (7)
17. Outcome of a competition (6)
19. Lose balance (6)
20. Pursue (5)
22. Domesticate (4)
24. Throw in the air (4)

HIDE AND SEEK

Solution on page 246.

In this puzzle you are looking for words linked to numbers associated with cats. We give you a cat clue in each case. The words are hidden in the sentences below and can be found by linking words or parts of words together.

1. Simba likes to climb on especially high trees
   (Clue: A cat has around 250 of these)

2. Emus clearly are native to Australia, which has no indigenous cat breed
   (Clue: One of 517 that a cat has)

3. Cats can be mysterious and quite ethereal by nature
   (Clue: A cat has around 30)

4. It is often said you don't choose a cat, it chooses you
   (Clue: This age in a cat is equivalent to 60 in a human)

5. The cats in the Israeli vessel in the harbour were excellent mousers
   (Clue: A cat is said to have nine of these)

MULTIPLE CHEWS

Solution on page 247.

Chew on these multiple-choice quiz questions, based on much-loved classic films.

1. General: Which film company has an opening sequence including a roaring lion?

   A 20th Century Fox

   B Metro-Goldwyn-Mayer

   C Paramount Pictures

   D Universal Pictures

2. 1951: In the original *Alice in Wonderland* film, what was the name of Alice's cat?

   A Diana

   B Dinah

   C Meena

   D Mia

3. 1961: After its performance in *Breakfast at Tiffany's*, the cat Orangey won the animal Oscar which is known by what name?

   A Cuddly

   B Cutey

   C Furry

   D Patsy

4. 1961: In the original film *One Hundred and One Dalmatians*, what was the name of the cat?

A Captain Tibbs

B Colonel Tibbs

C Corporal Tibbs

D Sergeant Tibbs

5. 1963: First appearing in *From Russia with Love*, what breed was the cat belonging to James Bond's nemesis Ernst Stavro Blofeld?

A British shorthair

B Burmese

C Persian

D Siamese

6. 1970: In the film *The Aristocats*, what was the name of the mother cat whom alley cat Thomas O'Malley helped to get back to Paris with her kittens?

A Baroness

B Countess

C Duchess

D Marchioness

7. 1978: What was the name of *The Cat from Outer Space*?

A Jack

B Jake

C Max

D Zach

8. 1979: What was the name of Ripley's pet cat in the film *Alien*?

A Eddie

B Jonesy

C Smithy

D Willie

9. 1990: In the film *Ghost*, what was the name of Molly's cat, who could still sense Sam after he died?

A Boyd

B Clyde

C Floyd

D Lloyd

10. 1992: In *Batman Returns*, Michael Keaton's second Batman movie, which actress played Catwoman?

A   Anne Hathaway

B   Eartha Kitt

C   Halle Berry

D   Michelle Pfeiffer

11. 1993: In the film *Hocus Pocus*, what was the name of the cat who had been previously been a boy before being turned into a cat by the three witches?

A   Binx

B   Jinx

C   Kinx

D   Minx

12. 1993: In *Homeward Bound: The Incredible Journey*, what was the name of the cat?

A   Sally

B   Sammy

C   Sandy

D   Sassy

MYSTIC MOG

Solution on page 247.

If you want to foresee the unseen, then send for Mystic Mog, the cat who knows it's not what you see that matters ... it's what you cannot see! There's a jumble of letters of the alphabet in the box.

What you need to find are the letters that do not appear. Use each missing letter once only to make the name of something that most cats like.

SIX FIX

Solution on page 247.

All answers have six letters and fit into the grid reading in a clockwise direction. We give you the starting point for the answer to Clue 1, but after that you have to work out in which hexagonal cell the answer begins.

CLUES

1. A cat skilled at catching small rodents

2. Runs after, follows

3. Changes to suit the situation

4. Supporter of a cause or charity

5. Feline with little or no colour

6. Gaudy spherical toy

7. Wild American cat

8. Coax, persuade

9. The most pleasant

10. Relating to the teeth

11. Holy, as cats in ancient Egypt were

12. Male feline

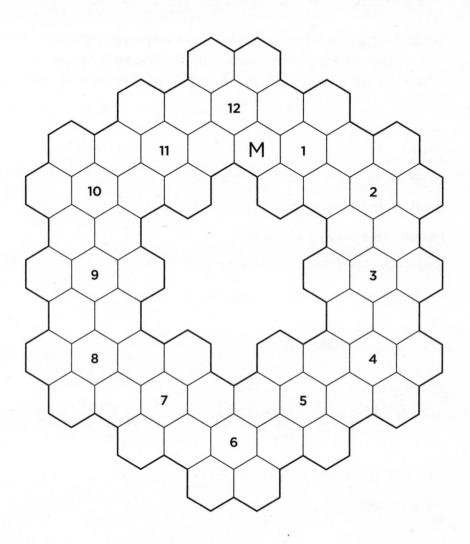

CAT COLLAR

Solution on page 248.

Solve the clues, which are in no particular order, and slot the seven-letter answers back into their correct places in the cat collar. The last letter of one answer is also the first letter of the next.

Answer 1 begins with a letter K.

CLUES

Break up the calm, which lively cats might do

Pursued stealthily

A common fish, a feline favourite

Enchant, captivate, which a sorceress's feline could succeed in doing

They make up a litter

CATWALK

Solution on page 248.

A straightforward crossword to stroll through.

ACROSS

8. Found refuge with a new family (7)
9. Characteristic (5)
10. Sneak, lurk (5)
11. Not large, not small (7)
12. Look out for (4)
13. Observing (8)
16. Was receptive to sound (8)
18. Curve the back (4)
21. Be daring (7)
23. Unhappy (5)
25. Cats like to climb them (5)
26. Unkempt (7)

DOWN

1. Hold tightly (4)
2. Select (6)
3. Scent (5)
4. Original thought (4)
5. Elongate (7)
6. An expedition to see large cats! (6)
7. Power, might (8)
12. Produce moisture in the mouth at the thought of food (8)
14. Consumed that food! (3)
15. Appeal or entreaty – to find new places for animals to live for example (7)
17. Sight, hearing, touch, etc. (6)
19. Relaxed, took time off (6)
20. Move (5)
22. Organs needed with regard to 16 Across (4)
24. Playthings (4)

TAGS

Solution on page 249.

The letters on the cat tags can be rearranged to form words. There are letters on individual tags, shared letters between two tags, and the space in the middle needs to be filled by a letter that is in all three tags.

You are looking for the names of three different things you might find in a cat first-aid kit.

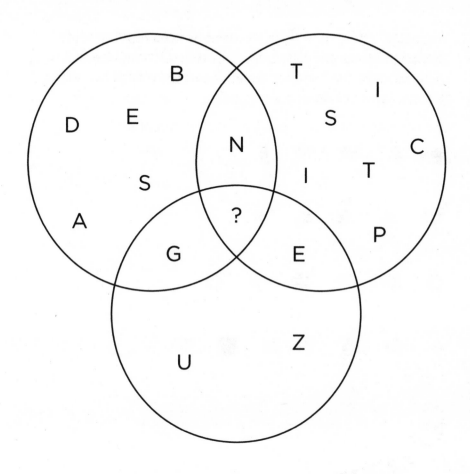

KEEP IN SHAPE

Solution on page 249.

Individual letters have been replaced by symbols. The first group stands for the letters M, O, G, G and Y – making the word MOGGY. The symbols remain constant throughout all the groups. What cat-related words do the other groups make?

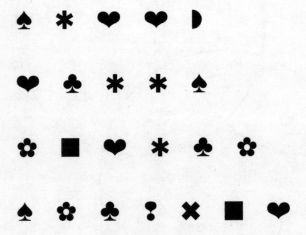

THAT'S MY CAT

Solution on page 249.

There is no doubting the breed of cat this owner has.
Rearrange all the letters in the personal name to form the
name of the type of cat.

C I L L A   H I N C H

CLUE:
One word

CAT CODES

Solution on page 250.

Answer the questions across in the upper grid. All answers have eight letters, except 9, which has two words of four letters.
Take the key-coded letters and place them in the lower grid. For example, the first letter you need is a W in square F8.

When you have finished, a proverb with a feline connection will be revealed.

CLUES

1. Bony structure of a cat containing around 250 bones

2. Without worries

3. Good looking

4. Vigilant, concentrating on its prey

5. Thoroughbred

6. An American breed which shares its name with an item of footwear for icy weather

7. Another word for striped, but a cat may enjoy this fishy food

8. A passage between buildings where a wild cat might lurk

9. Rear limbs (4.4)

10. Vision, which is very acute in a cat

	A	B	C	D	E	F	G	H
1								
2								
3								
4								
5								
6								
7								
8								
9								
10								

F8	A3	C1	C9		C4	F6	H2		C7	B4	F1	E3
B2	A4	B7	B10		H10	E4	G7		G3	D5	A2	H6
D6	B9	H7	D1		A5	H4	B3	H8				

ALL THE SEVENS

Solution on page 250.

The listed cat-linked words all contain seven letters. Fit them all back in the frame to read either across or down. One letter is keyed in. Take care! There is only one way to get all the words back in place.

BEWITCH

BURMESE

COLLARS

GROWN UP

HUNTING

OUTDOOR

PERSIAN

SCAMPER

SHOWING

SIAMESE

WHISKER

WILDCAT

FORWARD

Solution on page 251.

Cats slink forward ready to pounce. Move forward here to solve the puzzle. There are two clues each time and two solutions. The first clue is general and the second has a feline link.

The solutions are almost the same, the only difference being that in the second word the middle letter has moved forward in the alphabet.

1. Evergreen tree * Cat's coat
   (both words have three letters)

2. They sit on top of cricket wickets * Playthings
   (both words have five letters)

3. Dot and dash code * Prey
   (both words have five letters)

4. Portable lamp * One of the senses
   (both words have five letters)

TAKE A TUMBLE

Solution on page 251.

Cats don't always land unhurt if they take a tumble, but because of their powers of balance and coordination, they often come down to earth safe and sound.

In each of the sentences below, there are three words which are made up of the same letters. They are anagrams of each other. Can you tumble the letters around and work out what they are? Happy landing!

1. When we are outside, I try to steer my cat away from the trees. She loves climbing but I get a very terse response from other people when I have to go into their gardens to find her.

2. There are acres of space in the park. A wild-looking cat often races off at great speed, which causes a bit of a scare among those who enjoy a simple, gentle stroll.

3. My cats have the palest of coats; they are a pale grey. Their staple diet is fresh fish, and they clear their plates every time they eat.

GIVE ME FIVE!

Solution on page 251.

Solve the clues, which are listed at random. All the answers contain five letters. You have to fit the answers back in the frame, going either across or down.

There is a starter letter to help you on the way. There is only one way to fit all the words back.

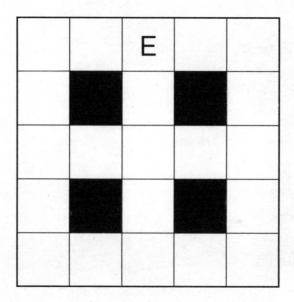

CLUES

Refreshing drink for a thirsty cat

Moves rapidly and suddenly

Type of cat

Receptacles to serve food in

Many different kinds and variety, all _____

Put your pet forward to be in a cat show

MULTIPLE CHEWS

Solution on page 252.

Chew on these multiple-choice quiz questions, based on cats in popular music.

1. The rockabilly group the Stray Cats had their first UK hit in 1979 with which song?

    A 'Rock This Town'
    B 'Runaway Boys'
    C 'Stray Cat Strut'
    D 'The Race is On'

2. The Dutch group Pussycat had a 1976 No. 1 with a song named after which US state?

    A California
    B Georgia
    C Mississippi
    D Virginia

3. Written for Euro 96, the football tournament being held in England in 1996, Frank Skinner and David Baddiel had a hit with 'Three Lions' alongside which group?

    A Hot House Flowers
    B Lightning Seeds
    C New Order
    D Squeeze

4. The Liverpool girl group Atomic Kitten were originally formed by members of which other Merseyside group, who also wrote some of their early songs?

A China Crisis

B Echo and the Bunnymen

c Frankie Goes to Hollywood

D Orchestral Manoeuvres in the Dark

5. Which singer had a 1965 hit with 'What's New Pussycat?'?

A Adam Faith

B Engelbert Humperdinck

c Tom Jones

D Tony Christie

6. Which former *X Factor* judge was also once a member of The Pussycat Dolls?

A Cheryl

B Kelly Rowland

c Nicole Scherzinger

D Tulisa

7. The 1960s/70s singer Cat Stevens changed his name in 1977 after converting to Islam to what?

A Ahmed Islam

B Ali Islam

C Mohammed Islam

D Yusuf Islam

8. Elton John had a 1972 hit with what kind of cat?

A Dinky Cat

B Honey Cat

C Honky Cat

D Monkey Cat

9. In the lyrics of the hit song 'Cool for Cats' by Squeeze, released in 1979, what speed were 'the Sweeney' going?

A Sixty

B Seventy

C Eighty

D Ninety

10. According to the 1974 song by Harry Chapin, covered by Ugly Kid Joe in 1992, the Cat's in the _____?

A Attic

B Cradle

C Garden

D Hat

11. 'The Lovecats' was a 1983 hit for which group?

A Echo and the Bunnymen

B The Cult

C The Cure

D The Psychedelic Furs

12. Which singer has cats called Meredith Grey, Olivia Benson and Benjamin Button?

A Dua Lipa

B Miley Cyrus

C Rihanna

D Taylor Swift

STRAY CAT

Solution on page 252.

The three letters in the word CAT have been replaced by question marks in the word below. Each question mark could be an A, a C or a T. It could be only one, two or three of those letters, or it could be more than one of any as well.

The other letters of the alphabet are in place. Can you replace the question marks with C, A or T to find the word?

We give you a clue to help you see that the stray cat makes it home.

? ? ? ? U S

CLUE:
Succulent plant

SEALPOINT

Solution on page 252.

Each answer contains FOUR letters. The first letter goes in
a numbered triangle, the second letter directly above it, the
third letter to the right and the fourth to the left. Answer words
interlock in the completed pointed grid.

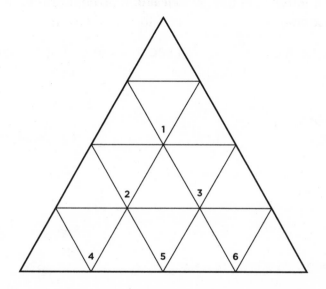

CLUES

1. Get close to

2. Makes a mistake

3. A cat's coat

4. Utilised, employed

5. Without restraint of any kind

6. Small rodents

NAME GAME

Solution on page 253.

Here's a list of some of the UK's favourite cat names in recent years. The words are hidden in the letter square. All words are in straight lines and can go horizontally, vertically and diagonally. They may read forwards or backwards.

There's one name in the list which is NOT hidden in the search. Which cat is it?

BELLA	JASPER	POPPY
BETTY	JESS	PRINCESS
BUBBLES	MAISY	PUMPKIN
CASPER	MEG	ROSIE
CLEO	MIA	SHADOW
FELIX	MILO	SIMBA
FLORENCE	MINNIE	SMOKEY
GINGER	MISTY	SNOWY
GINNY	PEBBLES	SOOTY
HOLLY	PHOEBE	SOX

```
P  O  C  A  S  P  E  R  J  I  X  O
H  E  Z  A  B  M  I  S  A  I  D  Y
D  C  B  M  P  M  N  Y  S  P  T  S
E  N  R  B  I  P  N  B  P  T  X  I
S  E  A  L  L  X  I  U  E  P  H  A
S  R  O  S  I  E  M  B  R  L  O  M
E  O  R  L  G  P  S  B  Z  A  L  P
C  L  E  O  K  X  O  L  M  Z  L  A
N  F  G  I  P  H  O  E  B  E  Y  J
I  R  N  A  E  Y  T  S  I  M  G  E
R  G  I  N  N  Y  Y  E  K  O  M  S
P  M  G  S  H  A  D  O  W  K  E  S
```

LEAP TO IT!

Solution on page 254.

Each of the 26 letters of the alphabet has been replaced by a number from 1 to 26. Work out which number represents which letter to complete the crossword-style grid, which has words reading across and down. You are given the letters in the word LEAP to start you off. 1 = L, 2 = E, 3 = A, 4 = P. Straight away you can fill in all the squares that contain the numbers 1, 2, 3 and 4.

Fill in the 1 to 26 grid with letters of the alphabet as you work them out.

When you have worked out the code, the letters 18, 22, 10, 18, 22, 20, 13, 2, 13, 17, 2, 1, 1, will spell out a cat coat colouring.

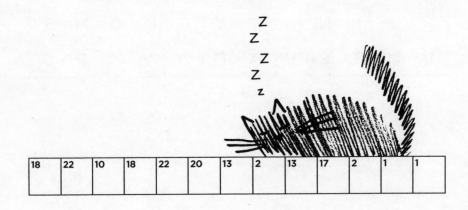

18	22	10	18	22	20	13	2	13	17	2	1	1

Codeword puzzle grid (numbers 1–26 to be decoded):

	13		13		5				17		12		25
1	20	18	18	2	10	13		18	2	10	10	3	20	16
	9		22		22		20		3		2		18	
1	2	3	4		22	26	16	2	10		2	3	18	13
			4		21		18				11		2	
24	23	20	2	18		13	2	3	1	4	22	20	16	18
	13		11		8		1		23		21			
6	2	18		8	22	1	1	3	10	13		22	1	11
			4		3		20		25		7		3	
4	3	10	2	16	18	3	5	2		14	23	21	4	13
	16		10				2		8		10			
1	20	2	13		21	23	16	8	17		21	3	16	19
	21		20		2		18		3		2		2	
21	3	1	3	15	3	16		7	10	23	13	17	2	13
	1		16		1				21		2		11	

Key grid:

1	2	3	4	5	6	7	8	9	10	11	12	13
14	15	16	17	18	19	20	21	22	23	24	25	26

CLOCK WATCH

Solution on page 254.

In this puzzle each answer has eight letters. Write the answer words in the grid, with each first letter going in a numbered square. Then you have to decide whether to write the answer in a clockwise or anti-clockwise direction. All the answers have to interlock together.

CLUES

1. One of the cat's most important senses

2. Following and remembering a trail or path

3. Maintains equilibrium

4. Energetic or purposeful movement

5. A mite or a flea, for example

6. Without any sound whatsoever

7. Something which presents no threat to a cat is described thus

8. Regular inhabitant of a building

FORWARD

Solution on page 254.

Cats slink forward ready to pounce. Move forward here to solve the puzzle. There are two clues each time and two solutions. The first clue is general and the second has a feline link.

The solutions are almost the same, the only difference being that in the second word the middle letter has moved forward in the alphabet.

1. Little * Scent
   (both words have five letters)

2. Useful, convenient * Resilient, as cats can be
   (both words have five letters)

3. Burrows, pits * Provides with a permanent place to live
   (both words have five letters)

4. Has a craving for * Pursuers, trackers
   (both words have seven letters)

STRAY CAT

Solution on page 255.

The three letters in the word CAT have been replaced by question marks in the word below. Each question mark could be an A, a C or a T. It could be only one, two or three of those letters, or it could be more than one of any as well.

The other letters of the alphabet are in place. Can you replace the question marks with C, A or T to find the word?

We give you a clue to help you see that the stray cat makes it home.

S ? ? ? ? E R E D

CLUE:

Widely distributed

FELINE FIVES

Solution on page 255.

Solve the cat-based clues, which are listed at random.

Each five-letter answer starts in a space with an odd number (1, 3, 5, 7, 9 and 11) and ends in a space with an even number (2, 4, 6, 8, 10 and 12).

The letter in space 1 is C.

CLUES

This means there are red or cream tips to the hair

Colour of a witch's feline companion

Relating to the nose, a cat's is much more sensitive than a human's

Smell which a cat might recognise and follow

Breakfast, lunch and dinner are all these

Skulk, slink

FITTING IN

Solution on page 255.

We all hope that a newcomer to the home will fit in as one of the family. In this puzzle a word with a feline feel about it has to be fitted into the spaces so that the word becomes complete.

All the words in 1 need the same three-letter word, as do numbers 2 and 3. Three different words for three different sections.

1. A M _ _ _ U R

   C _ _ _ G O R Y

   F R _ _ _ R N A L

2. C U R _ _ _ T S

   S O P _ _ _ O

   G U A _ _ _ T E E

3. V O L L _ _ _ D

   G R _ _ _ S T

   S U R V _ _ _ D

SPLITS

Solution on page 255.

There is evidence that the history of cats goes back to ancient civilisations. The names of places linked to some of them have been divided into a line of letters.

Can you work out the names of the two civilisations in each case? 1 is two of four letters, 2 is two of five letters, and in 3 there are two six-letter names.

The letters read in chronological order.

1 R S O M I A M E

2 E J G A P Y P T A N

3 C P E Y R P R S U S I A

NINE LIVES

Solution on page 255.

Nine boxes. Nine different letters of the alphabet. Solve the cunning clues and write the letters in the appropriate spaces in the grid.

When all nine letters are in place, the name for cats with a thick, soft fur is created.

CLUES

1. Tinkling, jingling like a bell on a cat's collar

   8 7 3 4 7 3 4

2. Dividing or apportioning food or accommodation

   9 5 6 8 7 3 4

3. Large amounts of fish – just what cats ordered!

   9 5 2 6 1 9

1	2	3	4	5	6	7	8	9

MYSTIC MOG

Solution on page 256.

If you want to foresee the unseen, then send for Mystic Mog, the cat who knows it's not what you see that matters ... it's what you cannot see! There's a jumble of letters of the alphabet in the box.

What you need to find are the letters that do not appear. Use each missing letter once only to make the name of something that most cats don't like.

SHADOW PLAY

Solution on page 256.

Answer the questions going across in the top grid. All answers have seven letters, other than question 1. When the top grid is complete, take the letters in the shaded squares and place them vertically, one below the other, in the lower grid.

When you have completed the lower grid, a famous expression with a feline connection will be revealed.

CLUES

1. Plaything (3) * Part of the mouth which holds the teeth (3)

2. Pillow-like accessory to pamper a cat

3. The climbing down from a tree

4. Luxury, ease, maybe provided by Question 2

5. Alleviate an itch

6. All muddled up, like lots of balls of wool

7. Shield from danger

8. Material a cat collar is made from

9. Breed of Asian cat first exhibited at the Crystal Palace in the late 19th century

10. Occupation of Pat, who had a cat called Jess

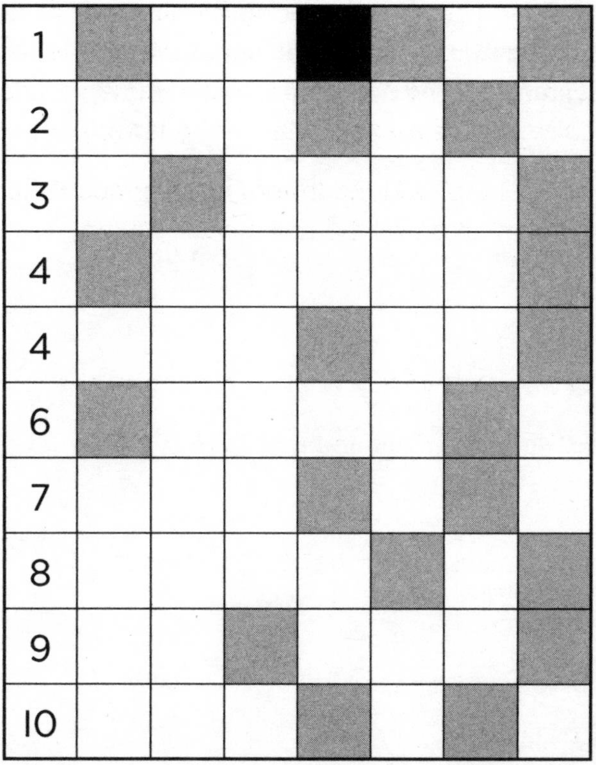
1
2
3
4
4
6
7
8
9
10

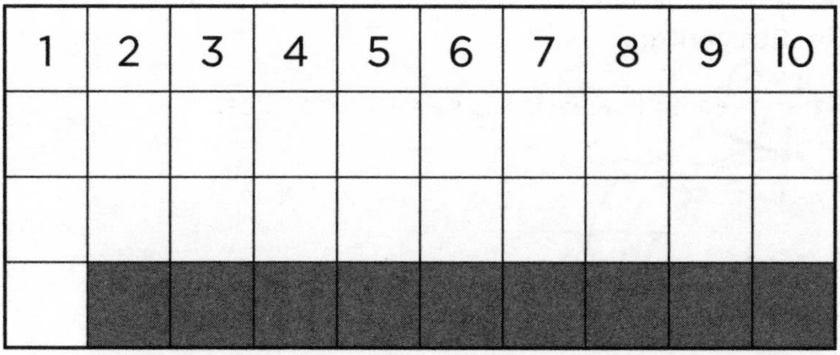
1 2 3 4 5 6 7 8 9 10

SHADY SEVENS

Solution on page 256.

Place all the listed seven-letter words to read across the grid
in such an order that the diagonal line of letters in the shaded
seven spaces forms the name of a breed of cat.

AGILITY

CAT FLAP

HEALTHY

OUTSIDE

PROWLED

SIT DOWN

STROKED

1						
2						
3						
4						
5						
6						
7						

MULTIPLE CHEWS

Solution on page 257.

Chew on these multiple-choice quiz questions, all about cats in literature.

1. In the *Meg and Mog* books by Helen Nicoll, Mog is a striped cat but what is Meg?

   A Farmer

   B Shopkeeper

   c Vampire

   D Witch

2. *Old Possum's Book of Practical Cats* was written by which author?

   A A.A. Milne

   B C.S. Lewis

   c E.B. White

   D T.S. Eliot

3. *Mog the Forgetful Cat*, the first in the Mog series of books, and *The Tiger Who Came to Tea* were written by which children's author?

   A Jacqueline Wilson

   B Judith Kerr

   c Judy Blume

   D Julia Donaldson

4. The 1957 book written by Dr Seuss, later turned into a 2003 film, was called *The Cat in the* _____?

A   Cradle

B   Garden

c   Hat

D   Suit

5. *The Tale of Tom Kitten* was written by which author?

A   Beatrix Potter

B   E. Nesbit

c   Enid Blyton

D   Roald Dahl

6. In *The Owl and the Pussy-Cat* by Edward Lear, which bird married them the next day?

A   Chicken

B   Duck

c   Goose

D   Turkey

7. In the children's books by Lynley Dodd, what is the name of the cat?

A Blinky Malinki
B Pinky Malinki
c Slinky Malinki
D Stinky Malinki

8. *Cat on a Hot Tin Roof* is a 1955 play, later turned into a 1958 film, written by which American playwright?

A Arthur Miller
B Eugene O'Neill
c Tennessee Williams
D Thornton Wilder

9. Tigger is one of the friends of which fictional bear?

A Balou
B Paddington
c Rupert
D Winnie-the-Pooh

10. In *Harry Potter and the Prisoner of Azkaban*, Hermione Granger buys a cat by what name?

A Crookshanks

B Fuzzclaw

c Snowy

D Tufty

11. In *The Chronicles of Narnia*, Aslan is what type of big cat?

A Jaguar

B Leopard

c Lion

D Tiger

12. In *Life of Pi,* written by Yann Martel, what name is given to the tiger?

A Peter Parker

B Richard Parker

c Thomas Parker

D William Parker

CAT COLLAR

Solution on page 257.

Solve the clues, which are in no particular order, and slot the seven-letter answers back into their correct places in the cat collar. The last letter of one answer is also the first letter of the next.

Answer 1 begins with a letter R.

CLUES

Drinking milk or water from a bowl

Describes ears with sharp tips

Adult (5.2)

Hand over a cat to its new home

Breed of American cat, which shares its name with a child's toy

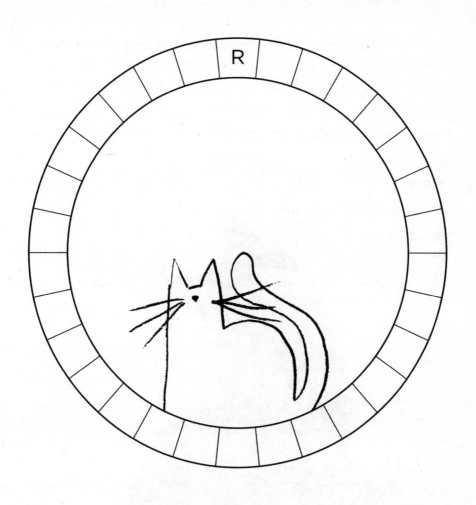

ALPHAGRAMS

Solution on page 257.

Famous people have been the most devoted cat owners throughout history. Famous names and those of their feline friends have had the letters in their names mixed up and rearranged in alphabetical order.

Can you work them all out? We also give you a clue about the identity of the celebrity.

1. C K O S S

B C I I L L N N O T
(former US President)

2. I M O S T U

A E I L M M N N O O R R Y
(famous blonde actress)

3. B B B E E E L U Z

A A I K M N R T W
(American novelist)

CRYPTI-CAT

Solution on page 258.

A cat-based crossword with a cryptic twist.

ACROSS

3. Peels back state of relaxation (5)
6. Step around animals kept in the house (4)
7. Begin to wake suddenly from a catnap (5)
8. The tale apparently contains a cat's jump (4)
10. It goes before melon and polo and quenches a thirst (5)
14. Part of a cat's house with sufficient space (4)
15. Myself married? The cat cried softly! (5)
16. Term of affection to your pet can be costly (4)
17. Notices markings on a Bengal cat (5)

DOWN

1. Magic made by a witch and her cat for a short while (5)
2. It's the final piece of bedding for the pets (5)
4. Group of newborn kittens leave behind unwanted items? (6)
5. Hears, in short, using these (4)
9. Pet ran round her dam (6)
11. Wandering cat given a dog's name? (5)
12. Clever cat is well dressed and tidy in appearance (5)
13. Look after a feline found in a castle (4)

TAGS

Solution on page 258.

The letters on the cat tags can be rearranged to form words. There are letters on individual tags, shared letters between two tags, and the space in the middle needs to be filled by a letter that is in all three tags.

You are looking for the names of three different cats from Disney movies, two from *The Aristocats* and one from *Cinderella*.

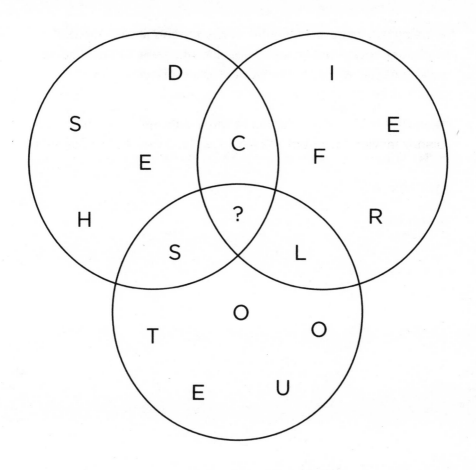

SHADY SEVENS

Solution on page 259.

Place all the listed seven-letter words to read across the grid
in such an order that the diagonal line of letters in the shaded
seven spaces forms the name of a breed of cat.

BRUSHED   RECLINE

HUNTING   ROAMING

KITTENS   STRETCH

PURPOSE

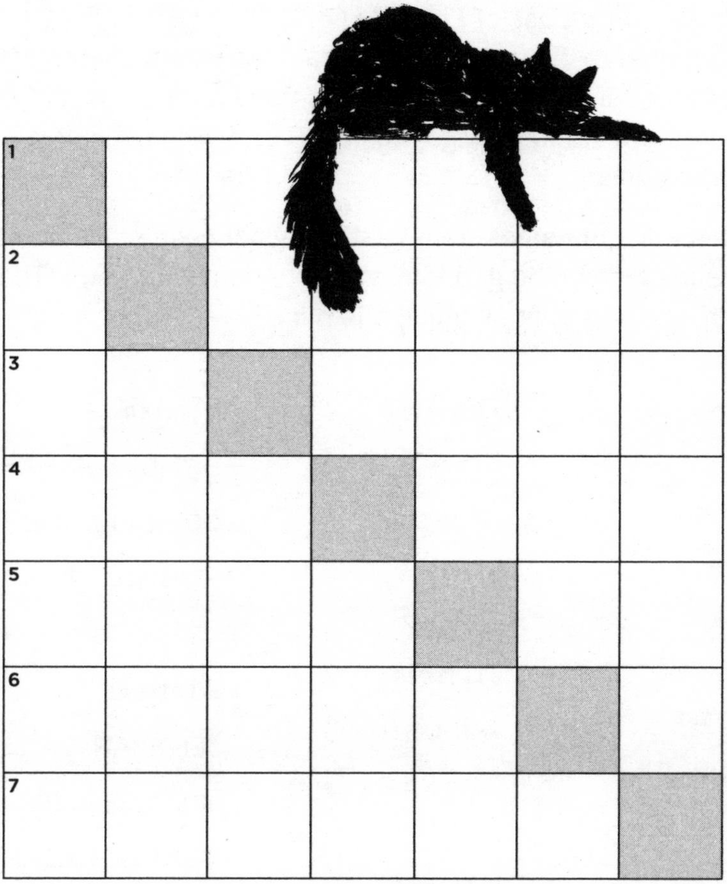
1
2
3
4
5
6
7

OLD POSSUM

Solution on page 259.

In *Old Possum's Book of Practical Cats*, the poet T.S. Eliot created a fantastic feline world of cats with great characters and wonderful names. The work was used for the basis of the Andrew Lloyd Webber stage musical *Cats*, which became a global success.

Here is a list of names from Eliot's original poems. Fit all the words in place in the grid to read either across or down. There is only one way to fit all the words back.

3 LETTERS

GUS

4 LETTERS

NAME

5 LETTERS

PETER

PLATO

6 LETTERS

ALONZO

GEORGE

MORGAN

VICTOR

7 LETTERS

ADMETUS

DEMETER

ELECTRA

8 LETTERS

AUGUSTUS

JELLICLE (*Cats*)

10 LETTERS

BILL BAILEY

GROWLTIGER

MUNKUSTRAP

11 LETTERS

BOMBALURINA

GRIDDLEBONE

MUNGOJERRIE

12 LETTERS

JENNYANYDOTS

MISTOFFELEES

RUMPELTEAZER

RUM TUM TUGGER

13 LETTERS

SKIMBLESHANKS

14 LETTERS

OLD DEUTERONOMY

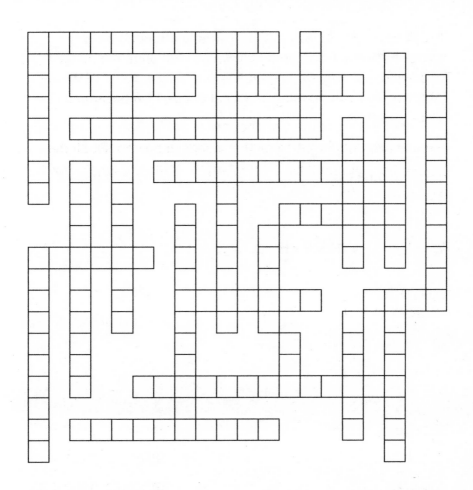

STRAY CAT

Solution on page 260.

The three letters in the word CAT have been replaced by question marks in the word below. Each question mark could be an A, a C or a T. It could be only one, two or three of those letters, or it could be more than one of any as well.

The other letters of the alphabet are in place. Can you replace the question marks with C, A or T to find the word?

We give you a clue to help you see that the stray cat makes it home.

? ? ? I V ? ? E D

CLUE:

Triggered, set in motion

MULTIPLE CHEWS

Solution on page 260.

Chew on these multiple-choice quiz questions, based on cartoon cats.

1. In the *Tom and Jerry* cartoons, what was the name of the bulldog?

A Butch

B Rover

c Samson

D Spike

2. Sylvester the Cat, who was always chasing Tweetie Pie, has what colour of nose?

A Black

B Blue

c Pink

D Red

3. In the *Top Cat* cartoons, one of the alley cats was called what?

A Barney the Ball

B Benny the Ball

c Billy the Ball

D Bobby the Ball

4. The designer of the fictional character Hello Kitty is what nationality?

A American

B Canadian

C Japanese

D Korean

5. In the Hanna-Barbera cartoons, what colour was Snagglepuss?

A Blue

B Green

C Pink

D Yellow

6. What is the name of Postman Pat's cat?

A Bess

B Jess

C Ness

D Tess

7. In 1919, the animated short film *Feline Follies* featured the first appearance of which cat?

A Felix

B Garfield

c Sylvester

D Tom

8. The 1970s animated TV series *Roobarb and Custard* told of the friendly rivalry between Custard, a pink cat, and Roobarb from next door, who was what type of animal?

A Bird

B Cat

c Dog

D Rabbit

9. What is the name of the pet cat in *The Simpsons*?

A Cannonball

B Fireball

c Furball

D Snowball

10. What was the name of the cat who appeared in cartoons with the two mice Pixie and Dixie?

A Mr Boots

B Mr Jinks

C Mr Tibbs

D Mr Whiskers

11. What is Garfield's favourite food?

A Burgers

B Fish and chips

C Lasagne

D Spaghetti bolognese

12. In the 1940 animated film *Pinocchio*, what was the name of Geppetto's pet cat?

A Angelo

B Fernando

C Figaro

D Ringo

CAT'S CRADLE

Solution on page 260.

The letters in SEVEN words below have been rearranged in alphabetical order. Can you put the letters back in their correct order and slot them in the grid?

The central shaded column reading down and 4 across are times of day. The other words are linked to daily feline routines.

1. B E L M R S U

2. D E N O O S Z

3. G I N P R R U

4. E E G I N N V

5. D E E I R S S

6. I G N N N R U

7. D E G I L M N

1						
2						
3						
4						
5						
6						
7						

FELINE FIVES

Solution on page 261.

Solve the cat-based clues, which are listed at random.

Each five-letter answer starts in a space with an odd number (1, 3, 5, 7, 9 and 11) and ends in a space with an even number (2, 4, 6, 8, 10 and 12).

The letter in space 1 is L.

CLUES

Not lavender, but a very pale dusky colour

Listens and responds

Shy, fearful

Expect, anticipate, a prey perhaps

Made domesticated, stopped from being wild

A breed referred to as chocolate is a shade of this colour

QUIZ CROSSWORD

Solution on page 261.

Solve the answer to each question in order to complete the grid.

ACROSS

3. What is the opposite of smooth to describe cats' hair? (5)
7. Which word for a fabric is the US name for a cat colouring? (6)
8. Which wild feline is native to South America? (6)
10. Which cat's prey is to be found in country meadows? (5.5)
11. What is a male feline parent called? (4)
12. Which mouse was always getting the better of Tom? (5)
13. Cats enjoy climbing. What is another word for climbing? (9)
16. What are the victors at cat shows called? (7)
21. What is another name for being grown up? (9)
22. What colour do the Americans call a brown Burmese? (5)
23. Which bones are attached to a cat's breastbone and sternum? (4)
24. What is a robber of buildings called, who is not necessarily a feline thief? (3.7)
26. What moisture forms in the mouth when a cat is ready to have food? (6)
27. What describes a shiny coat? (6)
28. What colour is an albino? (5)

DOWN

1. On old sailing boats there was often a ship's cat to keep the sailors company. What is another word for sailor? (7)
2. What is the first name of Mrs Clinton, who had a cat called Socks? (7)
3. What is an alternative word for wander? (4)
4. What is a house and also a refuge? (4)
5. What kind of coastal destination provides a holiday for Orlando, The Marmalade Cat? (7)
6. What word means 'bellowing' when referring to a lion or tiger? (7)
9. Which leading pantomime character is a cat dressed in spectacular footwear? (4.2.5)
14. Which organs in cats allow them to detect sounds to a much greater extent than humans? (4)
15. If a cat is pescatarian, what is part of its diet? (4)
17. Who would be in charge of the ship noted in 1 Down? (7)
18. Which stretchy ribbon is often attached to a cat's toy? (7)
19. What is the capital of the country where the Siamese cat originated? (7)
20. What does a cat do by licking? (7)
24. What is the sharp talon of a cat called? (4)
25. What is another word for encourage? (4)

SIX FIX

Solution on page 262.

All answers have six letters and fit into the grid reading in a clockwise direction. We give you the starting point for the answer to Clue 1, but after that you have to work out in which hexagonal cell the answer begins.

CLUES

1. Types of pedigree cats

2. Cat toy which makes a sound when shaken

3. Another toy; you crawl through this one!

4. Canned, as much cat food is

5. Urban areas where feral felines go hunting

6. Goes in

7. Brought up, raised

8. Place of safety

9. Led the way, maybe to 8

10. Coy, calm and composed

11. Pressed against, as when a cat spreads its scent

12. Scattered fragments from when a kitten has been boisterous

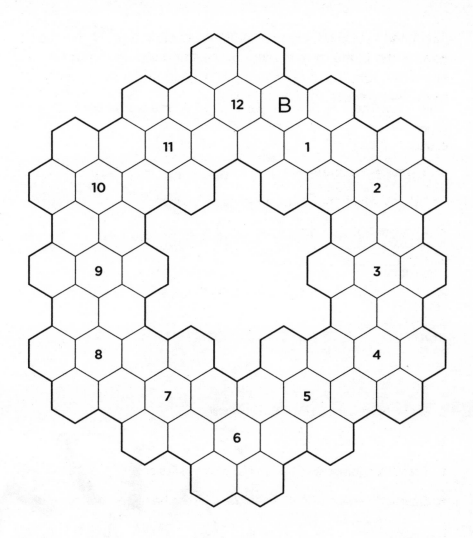

ALL THE SEVENS

Solution on page 262.

The listed cat-linked words all contain seven letters. Fit them all back in the frame to read either across or down. One letter is keyed in.

Take care! There is only one way to get all the words back in place.

CATTERY

CHEETAH

CONTROL

CUSHION

HEALTHY

PLAYFUL

POSTURE

PROTECT

PROWLED

SNUGGLE

STAMINA

STRETCH

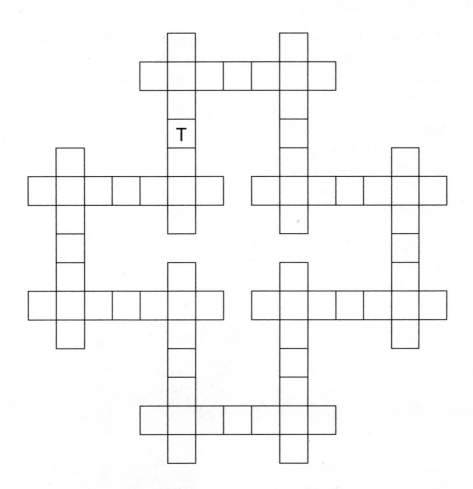

MYSTIC MOG

Solution on page 263.

If you want to foresee the unseen, then send for Mystic Mog, the cat who knows it's not what you see that matters ... it's what you cannot see! There's a jumble of letters of the alphabet in the box.

What you need to find are the letters that do not appear. Use each missing letter once only to make the name of something that most cats like.

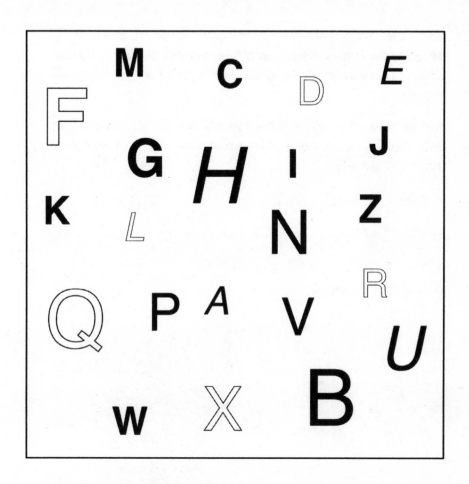

CAT COLLAR

Solution on page 263.

Solve the clues, which are in no particular order, and slot the seven-letter answers back into their correct places in the cat collar. The last letter of one answer is also the first letter of the next.

Answer 1 begins with a letter E.

CLUES

A Disney cat with a royal title

Took pleasure in

Green, canine companion of Custard the pink cat

Run around playfully

One of many used to make a brush

A TO Z

Solution on page 264.

Here's an A to Z of cat-related words (minus an X!). The words are hidden in the letter square. All words are in straight lines and can go horizontally, vertically and diagonally. They may read forwards or backwards.

There is one word that appears twice. Can you track it down?

ADVENTURE	JOYFUL	SEEK
BOUND	KNOW	TRANQUIL
COAT	LEAP	UNIQUE
DISREGARD	MAGNIFICENT	VISION
ENCHANT	NATURAL	WANDER
FUN	OUTSIDE	YAWN
GRACEFUL	PROWL	ZEST
HEADSTRONG	QUIETLY	
INTELLIGENT	REST	

I	E	L	A	R	U	T	A	N	W	E	D	K	U	G
S	N	U	G	N	O	R	T	S	D	A	E	H	V	C
Z	U	T	Q	T	N	A	H	C	N	E	N	I	L	T
E	D	S	E	I	L	N	I	P	S	O	S	D	U	S
S	T	A	P	L	N	Q	L	W	H	I	X	N	E	E
T	D	A	E	B	L	U	F	Y	O	J	I	R	V	R
P	E	D	O	G	Y	I	A	N	U	Q	U	E	L	T
L	U	R	N	Z	E	L	G	A	U	T	H	O	U	D
K	H	A	Z	U	P	E	T	E	N	I	L	E	F	O
M	A	G	N	I	F	I	C	E	N	T	E	D	E	R
O	P	E	Z	A	R	O	V	U	I	T	N	I	C	H
F	O	R	S	B	A	D	Y	Y	O	U	M	S	A	D
L	E	S	O	T	A	P	A	R	O	L	Q	T	R	E
H	U	I	C	W	U	L	W	B	E	R	E	U	G	D
M	P	D	E	E	L	O	N	G	E	S	W	O	N	K

MULTIPLE CHEWS

Solution on page 264.

Chew on these multiple-choice quiz questions, a test of your general cat knowledge.

1. What is the name of the cat who has lived at No. 10 Downing Street since 2011?

    A Larry

    B Lenny

    c Leroy

    D Louie

2. Tardar Sauce, the cat who became an American internet celebrity, had what nickname?

    A Crabby Cat

    B Cranky Cat

    c Grouchy Cat

    D Grumpy Cat

3. Choupette, the blue-cream tortie Birman cat, belonged to which fashion designer?

    A Giorgio Armani

    B Karl Lagerfeld

    c Ralph Lauren

    D Yves Saint Laurent

4. What is the collective name for a group of kittens?

A   Candle

B   Clutter

C   Huddle

D   Kindle

5. The Sphynx cat breed has no what?

A   Claws

B   Eyelids

C   Fur

D   Tail

6. Tabby cats got their name from a district in which city?

A   Baghdad

B   Beirut

C   Damascus

D   Tehran

7. After being elected in 1998, a cat called Stubbs was the mayor of a town for 20 years in which US state?

A Alaska

B Hawaii

C New Mexico

D Tennessee

8. How many cheek whiskers does a cat generally have?

A 16

B 20

C 24

D 28

9. What name was given to the cat who reportedly survived the sinking of three ships during the Second World War?

A Unsinkable Sam

B Unsinkable Sid

C Unsinkable Ted

D Unsinkable Tom

10. Tabby and Dixie were thought to be the first cats to live in the White House with which US President?

A Abraham Lincoln

B Andrew Jackson

c George Washington

D John Adams

11. The longest ever cat was over four feet long, a Maine Coon from Nevada with what name?

A Bluey

B Huey

c Louie

D Stewie

12. Which big cat cannot roar?

A Cheetah

B Leopard

c Lion

D Tiger

SEALPOINT

Solution on page 265.

Each answer contains FOUR letters. The first letter goes in a numbered triangle, the second letter directly above it, the third letter to the right and the fourth to the left. Answer words interlock in the completed pointed grid.

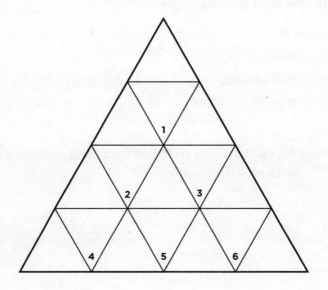

CLUES

1. Nourishment

2. Lazy, inactive

3. Dish for Clue 1

4. Look for, search

5. Alternatively

6. Possesses

NUMBER SUMS

Solution on page 265.

Work out the number sums with a difference below. Cat-linked calculations and mathematical magic combine.

A. Add the number of 'lives' a trio of cats might have plus the number of tails on two lynxes.

B. The year the movie *Cats* was released plus the number of letters in the name of a group of lions.

C. The number of letters in the name of Beatrix Potter's Kitten plus the number of letters in the name of the creature who went to sea with the Pussycat in a beautiful pea-green boat.

CRYPTI-CAT

Solution on page 266.

A cat-based crossword with a cryptic twist.

ACROSS

3. Main man at the wedding gives cat a tidy-up (5)
6. Overcome decisively a cat's method of washing (4)
7. Crazy marketing chaps rewrite the rules (5)
8. Puts an end to metal containers of cat food (4)
10. Stories, we hear, not belonging to Manx cats (5)
14. Takes food when out east (4)
15. Incorrect spelling in diary makes milk products (5)
16. Sounds like the streak of coloured fur should be prohibited (4)
17. Carelessly flip a coin making feline-friendly protection from the sun (5)

DOWN

1. Describes the arts concerning a witch's cat? (5)
2. Distribute American coins attracting cats (5)
4. Ruffle the fur behind the French (6)
5. Flurry of snow possesses a pet (4)
9. Bastet not scared to be this in ancient Egypt (6)
11. It's the devil of a name for a cat! (5)
12. Private words revealed as I deal with my pet (5)
13. Immerse and wash your cat in a Somerset city (4)

TAGS

Solution on page 267.

The letters on the cat tags can be rearranged to form words. There are letters on individual tags, shared letters between two tags, and the space in the middle needs to be filled by a letter that is in all three tags.

You are looking for the names of three different cats from T.S. Eliot's *Old Possum's Book of Practical Cats*.

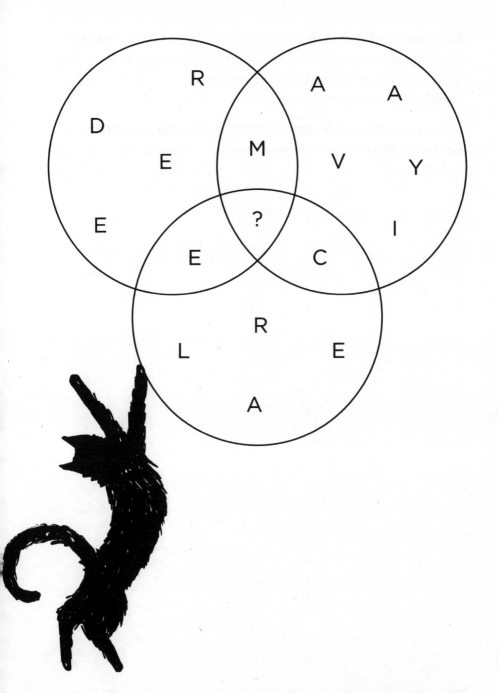

CAT BASKET

Solution on page 267.

The cats need to go in their basket. In the letter box the word CATS appears along with three other words of four letters. The words appear in straight lines of letters that can go across, back, up, down or diagonally.

Use these words to fill the empty basket by creating a word square in which the words read the same going across and down.

I	E	C	A	L	Z
W	D	W	A	W	U
E	A	E	D	T	W
Y	L	I	A	W	S
J	S	Y	R	E	W
C	J	S	E	A	T

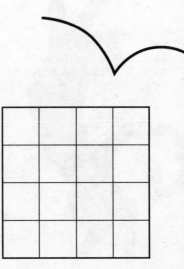

WHO AM I?

Solution on page 267.

Use the clues in the rhyme to find the letters to name
a famous feline.

Use all the clues, and spell out my name.

My first is in BALL
But isn't in BAT

My second is in CALL
And also in CAT

My third is in RACE
But isn't in CHASE

My fourth is in CARE
But isn't in SPACE

My fifth is in EYES
But isn't in SAME

NUMBER NAMES

Solution on page 268.

What's a cat worth? They are all beyond price, of course. However, with these cats we have taken the letters from their names and given them each a value.

Six different letters in all are used. The numbers allocated are between 1 and 6. The total of each name is worked out by adding individual letters together.

B O B = 4

B O B B Y = 8

T O B Y = 1 0

T A B B Y = 1 4

What is B A R R Y worth?

KEEP IN SHAPE

Solution on page 268.

Individual letters have been replaced by symbols. The first group stands for the letters P, E, R, S, I, A and N – making the word PERSIAN. The symbols remain constant throughout all the groups. What cat-related words do the other groups make?

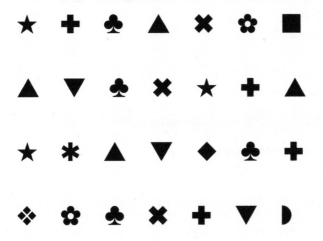

CAT CODES

Solution on page 268.

Answer the questions across in the upper grid. All answers have eight letters. Take the key-coded letters and place them in the lower grid. For example, the first letter you need is an A in square A1.

When you have finished, a proverb with a feline connection will be revealed.

CLUES

1. Taking on a rescue cat as part of the family

2. A fictional cat from this county was famous for grinning

3. This breed is sometimes called a poodle cat because of its curly coat (5.3)

4. A special midday meal, for a person or a feline

5. A red brown coat, or a favourite spice

6. Search for food

7. This goes before shell to describe a coat with mixed patches of colour

8. They protect from wind, rain and cold

9. Describes a family pet

10. Activity, motion, gait

	A	B	C	D	E	F	G	H
1								
2								
3								
4								
5								
6								
7								
8								
9								
10								

A1		A2	E5	D7		G9	G10		H1	A4	D3	D6	F8	E9
A5	C6	A7	D4	E2	D10	G7		E3	C1		F5	F7	B6	C8

MULTIPLE CHEWS

Solutions on page 269.

Chew on these multiple-choice quiz questions, based on modern movie cats.

1. 1994: In *The Lion King*, what is the name of the main character who is a lion cub at the beginning of the film?

A Mufasa

B Nala

C Samba

D Simba

2. 1997: In the *Austin Powers* series of films, what is the name of Dr Evil's cat?

A Mr Bigglesworth

B Mr Digglesworth

C Mr Jigglesworth

D Mr Tigglesworth

3. 1999: In *The Matrix*, Neo sees what as an example of déjà vu, which makes him realise there is a glitch in the Matrix?

D Black-and-white cat

B Black cat

C Ginger cat

D White cat

4. 1999: What is the name of the cat in *Stuart Little*?

A Snowball

B Snowbell

c Snowdrop

D Snowfall

5. 2000: Robert De Niro has a cat called Mr Jinx in which film?

A *Analyze This*

B *Meet the Parents*

c *Showtime*

D *Wag the Dog*

6. 2001: In the *Harry Potter* films, Mrs Norris is a cat belonging to which character?

A Argus Filch

B Filius Flitwick

c Hermione Granger

D Severus Snape

7. 2001: In the film *Cats and Dogs*, what is the name of the Persian cat who is the main antagonist?

A Mr Crinkles

B Mr Sprinkles

C Mr Tinkles

D Mr Winkles

8. 2003: In *The Cat in the Hat*, which actor plays the eponymous character?

A Ben Stiller

B Jim Carrey

C Mike Myers

D Robin Williams

9. 2004: Which actor voiced Puss in Boots in *Shrek 2*, later being the main character in the 2011 film *Puss in Boots*?

A Antonio Banderas

B Eddie Murphy

C John Cleese

D Mike Myers

10. 2006: In the film *Over the Hedge*, Tiger, the cat, falls in love with Stella, who is what type of animal?

A   Rabbit

B   Raccoon

C   Skunk

D   Squirrel

11. 2008: What is the name of the cat in *Bolt*?

A   Midge

B   Milo

C   Missy

D   Mittens

12. 2016: In the true story about a homeless man befriending a cat in London, the title of the film is *A Street Cat Named ___*?

A   Bill

B   Bob

C   Dave

D   Tom

CRYPTI-CAT

Solution on page 270.

A cat-based crossword with a cryptic twist.

ACROSS

3. Search this cold landscape and tell off a mischievous kitten (5)
6. World famous musical concerning moving acts (4)
7. Type of cat sounds like he's on your side (5)
8. Crack a break in friendly relations (4)
10. Fume uncontrollably before the king concerning a bone (5)
14. Cat's somersault made of bread (4)
15. A how-to care for cats manual, possibly the work of an ex-Brownie (5)
16. Feline's outer body layer and the protective parts of some fruits (4)
17. Sounds like you produce musical notes putting things into practice (5)

DOWN

1. Twenty kittens! That's the result (5)
2. Stout stick to run a cat's home? (5)
4. Blush when describing a feature of a cat's coat (6)
5. The cat stretches out, but that's not the truth! (4)
9. Cat's body tissue gives net returns before a professor (6)
11. Shelter and shade providers moves to the beat (5)
12. Cat's stealthy movement on a badly prepared golf course (5)
13. Fruit sweet found in a cat's mouth? (4)

FELINE FRIENDS

Solution on page 270.

Four cat owners meet up. From the remarks made and the information given, can you discover the names of the people (A to D) and match them to their cats (1 to 4) and give the age of each cat?

Cat 1 is neither the oldest at six or the youngest at one

Cat 2 has a black coat but is not the cat called Jude

Cat 3 has a black coat but is not owned by Max

Cat 4 is called Pandora

Gentleman A says: "My cat is aged one. Celia's cat is not called Jude"

Lady B says: "My cat has a white coat"

Lady C says: "Marcus's cat is twice as old as my cat Peach"

Gentleman D says: "Katie's cat Tommy is aged five"

NINE LIVES

Solution on page 271.

Nine boxes. Nine different letters of the alphabet. Solve the cunning clues and write the letters in the appropriate spaces in the grid.

When all nine letters are in place, a word for successful felines is created.

CLUES

1. The word *gato* means cat in this language

   9 5 3 8 6 9 2

2. Funny, or a description of a cartoon strip like *Garfield*

   1 7 4 6 1

3. This is made up of metal links and can be used as a collar

   1 2 3 6 8

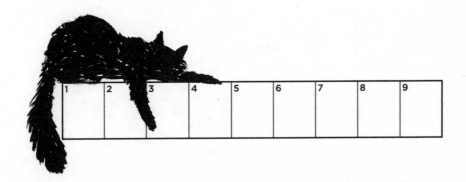

CLOCK WATCH

Solution on page 271.

In this puzzle each answer has eight letters. Write the answer words in the grid, with each first letter going in a numbered square. Then you have to decide whether to write the answer in a clockwise or anti-clockwise direction.

All the answers have to interlock together.

CLUES

1. They are high on a cat's head and are sensitive to sound (3, 5)

2. Not inside

3. Name or recognise, with the help of a tag

4. A miserable person, not necessarily a cat despite the name

5. A cat owner, but not its master

6. Keeping a cat clean

7. Nimble, skilled in exercise

8. The first word of Grizabella's song 'Memory' in *Cats;* a time on the clock!

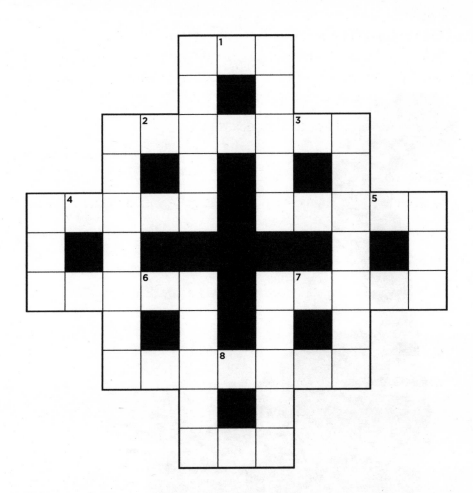

GIVE ME FIVE!

Solution on page 271.

Solve the clues, which are listed at random. All the answers contain five letters. You have to fit the answers back in the frame, going either across or down.

There is a starter letter to help you on the way. There is only one way to fit all the words back.

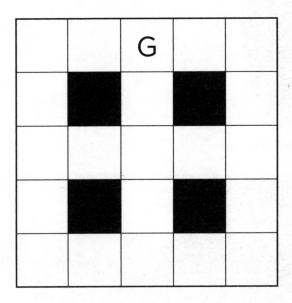

CLUES

Tidy and clean your pet

These are used to identify individual cats

Perhaps you can take some of these if you have nine lives!

Stares at, which most cats do very well

Another word for a claw

Large striped wild cat

FELINE FIVES

Solution on page 272.

Solve the cat-based clues, which are listed at random.

Each five-letter answer starts in a space with an odd number (1, 3, 5, 7, 9 and 11) and ends in a space with an even number (2, 4, 6, 8, 10 and 12).

The letter in space 1 is M.

CLUES

This western county precedes Rex in the name of a pedigree

Nimble, lithe

Lick to remove dirt

Shows signs of tiredness

Go in for, or enrol for a competition or show

Popular name for a cross-breed cat

SHADOW PLAY

Solution on page 272.

Answer the questions going across in the top grid. All answers have seven letters. When the top grid is complete, take the letters in the shaded squares and place them vertically, one below the other, in the lower grid.

When you have completed the lower grid, a question with a feline connection will be revealed.

When you look carefully at this question, do you notice anything unusual about it?

CLUES

1. Hair on the face of a cat, or part of a crystal radio set

2. Natural home

3. Strong, unbreakable substance a cat's bowl might be made of

4. Andrew Lloyd Webber's *Cats* is this type of entertainment

5. Unhurried, persevering, as in stalking prey

6. A small fish often tightly packed in a tin

7. 19th-century author Charles, who had a cat named Wilhelmina

8. Leave behind, forsake, as a neglected litter might be

9. Ahead, in the direction of your destination

10. Neckbands

FITTING IN

Solution on page 272.

We all hope that a newcomer to the home will fit in as one of the family. In this puzzle, a word with a feline feel about it has to be fitted into the spaces so that the word becomes complete.

All the words in 1 need the same three-letter word, as do numbers 2 and 3. Three different words for three different sections.

1. C O _ _ _ E D

   V E L _ _ _ Y

   _ _ _ O E D

2. P O _ _ _ I O N

   C A M P _ _ _ E

   D E P O _ _ _

3. _ _ _ L O N G

   I N _ _ _ I A T E

   R E _ _ _ B I S H

STRAY CAT

Solution on page 272.

The three letters in the word CAT have been replaced by question marks in the word below. Each question mark could be an A, a C or a T. It could be only one, two or three of those letters, or it could be more than one of any as well.

The other letters of the alphabet are in place. Can you replace the question marks with C, A or T to find the word?

We give you a clue to help you see that the stray cat makes it home.

V ? ? ? ? I O N

CLUE:

Holiday

SOLUTIONS

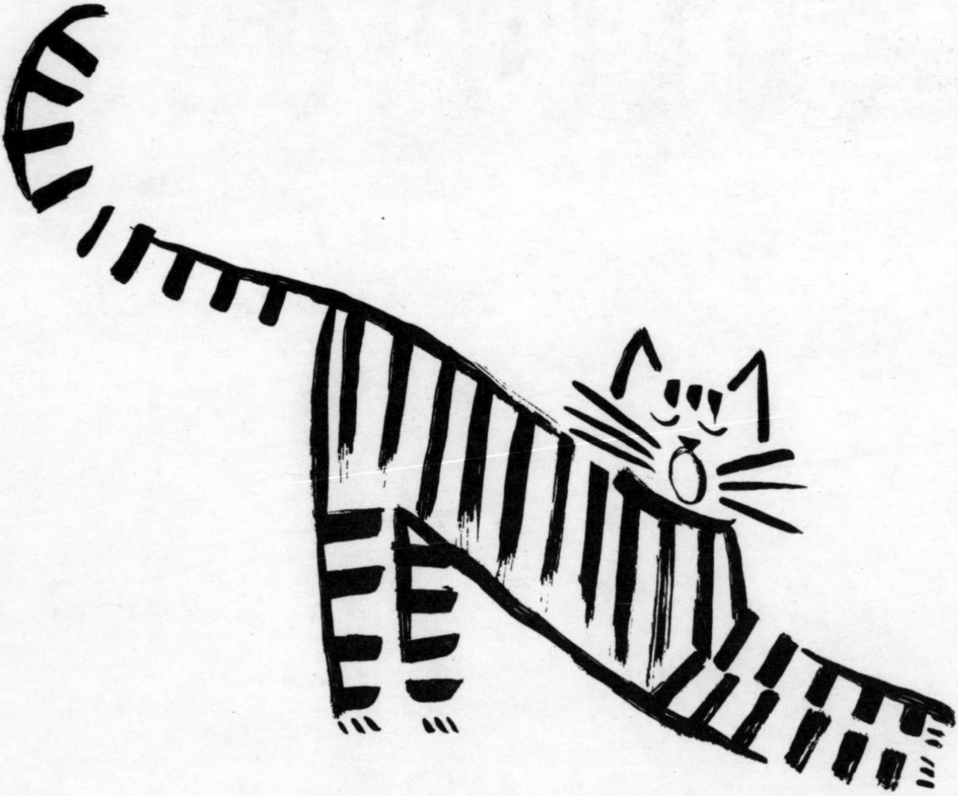

KEEP IN SHAPE

TRAY
STRAY
TOYS
TREAT

A TO Z

ELEGANT and KITTEN appear twice.

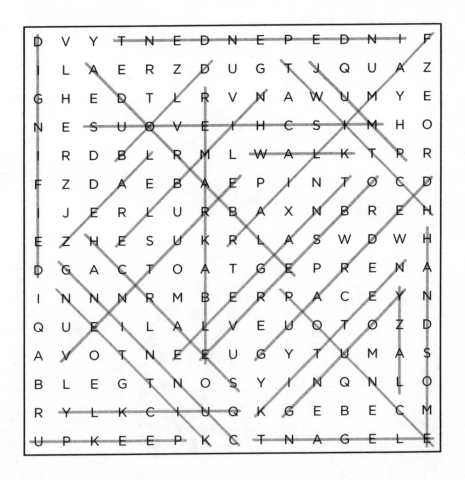

FITTING IN

1. Tom, 2. Lap, 3. Nap.

CAT BASKET

C	A	T	S
A	R	E	A
T	E	A	M
S	A	M	E

QUIZ CROSSWORD

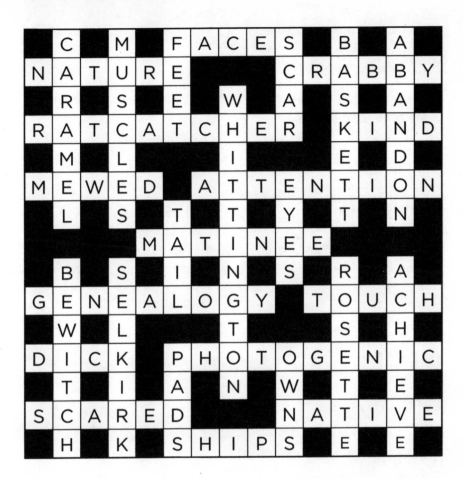

STRAY CAT

Catastrophic

NINE LIVES

1. Photos, 2. Teeth, 3. Brushes.

BUSTOPHER.

Bustopher Jones was a character in T.S. Eliot's *Old Possum's Book of Practical Cats*.

CLOCK WATCH

1. Armchair (C), 2. Fanciers (C), 3. Domestic (C), 4. Balinese (A), 5. Searched (A), 6. Rewarded (A), 7. Ancestor (A), 8. Selected (C).

CAT NAP

COCO – 70 minutes – Lounge.
MILO – 80 minutes – Hall.
MOLLY – 20 minutes – Kitchen.
POPPY – 30 minutes – Landing.
ROSIE – 40 minutes – Dining room.

SHADY SEVENS

1. Striped, 2. Nibbles, 3. Playful, 4. Climbed, 5. Baskets, 6. Fastest, 7. Posture.

SIAMESE is formed in the shaded diagonal.

SIX FIX

1. Feline, 2. Dining, 3. Fiddle, 4. Select, 5. Tiaras, 6. Praise, 7. Depend, 8. Cuddle, 9. Crouch, 10. Circle, 11. Frolic, 12. Forage.

THAT'S MY CAT

ABYSSINIAN

ALPHAGRAMS

1. *Cat on a Hot Tin Roof*, 2. *Cat Ballou*, 3. *What's New Pussycat?* 4. *Puss in Boots*, 5. *Dick Whittington and His Cat.*

CATWALK

B		H		P		R		L		A		C
E	D	U	C	A	T	E		E	A	R	T	H
L		N		W		I		I		O		A
L	I	T	H	E		R	E	S	C	U	E	R
		E		D			U		S			I
P	A	D	S		O	V	E	R	S	E	A	S
A			T		E		E					M
M	A	T	U	R	I	T	Y		G	A	L	A
P		H		A			S		M			
E	V	E	N	I	N	G		M	I	A	O	W
R		H		L		A		I		Z		A
E	V	A	D	E		M	O	T	H	E	R	S
D		T		D		E		E		D		H

FELINE FIVES

1-2. Miaow, **3-4.** Foods, **5-6.** Adult, **7-8.** Alley, **9-10.** Heart, **11-12.** Trait.

REHOMING

A completed crossword grid containing the words: VACCINATIONS, ADDRESS, VET, FORMS, SUITABLE, GUIDANCE, DETAIL, BEHAVIOUR, OWN, TEMPERAMENT, INDIVIDUAL, RESEARCH, RESCUE, MICROCHIP, EXERCISE, ADVICE, SUPPORT, CHARACTER, REWARDING, EMOTIONAL, HELP, CARE, MATCH, PREFERENCES, REGISTER, PET, CHANCE, ENQUIRES, ADOPT, COMMITMENT, QUESTIONS, NEEDS, HATE.

CAT COLLAR

1. Cattery, 2. Yearned, 3. Dustbin, 4. Nicosia, 5. Angelic.

HIDE AND SEEK

1. WAIN. Parliament Hill cat colony, in OttaWA IN Canada, closed in 2013.
2. MANET. I found my cat ToM AN ETernal problem, always trying to escape.
3. RENOIR. Chase the cat and climb that tree for a daRE? NO I Really meant it.
4. PICASSO. A lecture on cats is a wonderful toPIC AS SOmetimes happens.
5. GOYA. Some time aGO YArds of wool were unravelled by the kittens.

PET'S GARDEN

1. Catmint, 2. Acacia, 3. Carnation, 4. Chrysanthemum, 5. Nicotina, 6. Terracotta pots.

108 GIVE ME FIVE!

T	A	B	B	Y
E	█	L	█	E
A	R	O	M	A
C	█	O	█	R
H	I	D	E	S

CAT'S CRADLE

1. Scamper, 2. Behaved, 3. Ambling, 4. Sumatra, 5. Playing,
6. Escaped, 7. Meander.

MALAYAN and SUMATRA are formed in the shaded crosses.

MULTIPLE CHEWS

1. **D.** Vienna

2. **D.** *Pokémon*

3. **C.** *Glee*

4. **A.** Data

5. **D.** Zazzles

6. **B.** *Game of Thrones*

7. **A.** Advertising slogan (claiming that 8 out of 10 cats preferred a certain type of cat food)

8. **A.** Bagpuss

9. **C.** Salem

10. **C.** *The Gentle Touch*

11. **A.** Cat

12. **B.** Phoebe

MYSTIC MOG

The six missing letters are A, E, R, T and W.

Rearranged they make the word WATER.

THAT'S MY CAT

JAPANESE BOBTAIL

SPLITS

1. Blue, Seal,
2. Black, Cream,
3. Bronze, Silver.

SIX FIX

1. Angora, 2. Proper, 3. Prefer, 4. Define, 5. Orders, 6. Cosset,
7. Active, 8. Devote, 9. Warden, 10. Gnawed, 11. Pawing,
12. Awaken.

WHO AM I?

FELIX

The first letter could be an E or an F from the rhyme. The second, third and fourth have no option available. The fifth could be an I or an X. F and X are the only options to combine with the letters given.

FELIX is the name of the black-and-white cartoon cat who first appeared in a film in 1919. In the song about him, he famously 'kept on walking still'.

SEALPOINT

1. Call, 2. Flee, 3. Blue, 4. Pets, 5. Kept, 6. Jump.

KEPT SAFE

CHINCHILLAS is the coded word.

1	2	3	4	5	6	7	8	9	10	11	12	13
K	E	P	T	A	U	O	R	S	G	H	Z	W

14	15	16	17	18	19	20	21	22	23	24	25	26
B	C	N	M	Y	L	F	Q	V	J	I	X	D

Words formed, reading from left to right and top to bottom of the grid:

ACROSS:

Curious, Nametab, Kept, Chase, Tail, Alert, Companion, Rex, Perfect, Bed, Nocturnal, Purrs, Live, Scent, Pets, Watches, Yawning.

DOWN:

Cute, Litters, Quick, Laze, Resting, Calico, Camouflaged, Lie, Pick, Dear, Ear, Stretch, Jumping, Ocicat, Stray, Seek, Tiny.

SHADOW PLAY

1. Loudest, 2. Ancient, 3. Tomcats, 4. Take off, 5. Inherit, 6. Cheetah, 7. Check up, 8. Tabbies, 9. Tagging, 10. Showing.

The expression is: 'Let the cat out of the bag.' It is thought this might refer to unscrupulous traders who suggested an animal like a pig was in the bag when it was, in fact, a cat.

TAGS

TOP LEFT: Chocolate. **TOP RIGHT:** Platinum. **LOWER CIRCLE:** Chestnut.

The letter in the centre common to all tags is a T.

CLOCK WATCH

1. Cat Shows (C), **2.** Noah's Ark (C), **3.** Revisits (C), **4.** Wandered (C),
5. Wirehair (A), **6.** Adoption (A), **7.** Backbone (A), **8.** Sidewalk (A).

ALL THE SEVENS

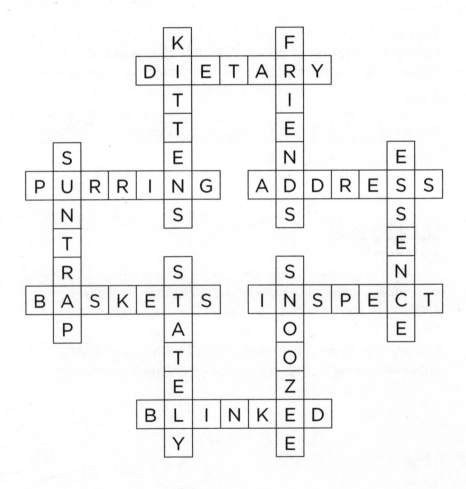

NUMBER NAMES

LOLA is worth 17. I = 1, M = 2, A = 3, L = 4, Y = 5, O = 6.

For MIA to be worth 6, the individual letters have to be 1, 2 and 3 in any order. The names MILLY and MOLLY contain the same letters, except one has an I and the other has an O. The difference in values is 5 (21 − 16 = 5). O must equal the value of I + 5. As 6 is the highest number, O must be 6 and I must be 1.

The value of MILO is 13. The I = 1 and the O = 6, which makes 7, leaving the combined M + L to equal the rest of the value. (13 − 7 = 6). From looking at MIA, the letter M is either a 2 or a 3. Both M and L cannot be 3, so the only option is for M = 2 and L = 4. A was also either 2 or 3, so that is now fixed as 3. 5 is the only number left to fix, so that must be Y.

LOLA = 4 + 6 + 4 + 3 = 17

CAT CODES

1. Champion, 2. Oriental, 3. Markings, 4. Victoria, 5. Holidays, 6. Whiskers, 7. Breeding, 8. Charcoal, 9. Platinum, 10. Moulting.

The proverb reads, 'All cats are grey in the dark,' meaning the hours of darkness disguise all distinguishing features.

CATWALK

WITH CAT-LIKE TREAD

```
S H L L O R T S N P J S
T A J U S A R P T E H M
R E U L L M E X R A Y K
A S I N I B A C D O L A
C N L S T L D O A A W K
K I T L H E W N W R G L
B E E P E E R C U S T E
P A V C R L U R K O T U
P R O O N E S A H C B S
J R S R M U E W A R I R
P T N U H F O L L O W U
S S E R G O R P A D E P
```

MULTIPLE CHEWS

1. **D.** 230
2. **B.** Isle of Man
3. **B.** Egyptians
4. **D.** Ypres
5. **A.** Tomcat
6. **C.** 18
7. **B.** Isaac Newton
8. **A.** Maine Coon
9. **C.** 3
10. **A.** *The Beano*
11. **C.** 38
12. **D.** Clowder

STRAY CAT

Incantation

KEEP IN SHAPE

MOUSE
SMELL
SLEEPS
SUPPLE

CRYPTI-CAT

S		S		S	C	A	R	E
P	A	W	S		R		E	
O		I		F	E	A	S	T
R	I	S	E		E		T	
T		H	A	P	P	Y		S
	T		T		S	O	F	T
T	R	A	I	N		U		E
	E		N		S	N	A	P
W	E	I	G	H		G		S

TAKE A TUMBLE

1. Cater, React, Trace.

2. Rescued, Secured, Reduces.

3. Andrew, Wander, Warned.

NUMBER SUMS

A. 0.
Bobcats don't have tails. Alice met the Cheshire cat. However, any number multiplied by zero is zero.

B. 80.
Tom and Jerry made their debut in 1940, as did Figaro in *Pinocchio.*

C. 17.
The year was 1970.

WHAT'S MY LINE?

1. Actor, **2.** Teacher, **3.** Accountant, **4.** Architect, **5.** Actuary, **6.** Cartoonist.

SEALPOINT

1. Dine, **2.** Vets, **3.** Knot, **4.** Espy, **5.** Step, **6.** Move.

FITTING IN

1. Lie, **2.** Hair, **3.** Ears.

FELIDAE CLOSE

1. Tigger, 2. Lily, 3. Snowy, 4. Milo, 5. Tom, 6. Flo.

NINE LIVES

1. Round, 2. Treat, 3. Cartoon.

UNDERCOAT

GIVE ME FIVE!

B	E	L	L	S
R	■	I	■	O
O	S	C	A	R
W	■	K	■	E
N	O	S	E	S

FOOD FOR THOUGHT

MR JONES – Fluffy – Sardines – Tabby.

MS KENT – Jerry – Tuna – Ginger.

MS LUCAS – Chloe – Kippers – Black.

MR MARTIN – Lucy – Chicken – White.

MS NEALE – Daisy – Liver – Grey.

CAT'S CRADLE

1. Groomed, 2. Hearing, 3. Stealth, 4. Kennedy, 5. Gingery,
6. Sleeker, 7. Playful.

ORANGEY and KENNEDY are formed in the shaded crosses.

CATWALK

B		R		S		F		R		S		V
R	O	U	G	H	E	R		E	X	T	R	A
E		N		A		E		P		A		C
D	R	O	O	P		E	L	A	S	T	I	C
		F		E				I		I		I
S	A	F	E		A	M	E	R	I	C	A	N
C			A		E		S				E
H	E	R	E	D	I	T	Y		O	W	N	S
E		E		V				C		O	
D	I	S	T	A	N	T		H	A	B	I	T
U		U		N		A		A		B		O
L	I	L	A	C		M	U	S	C	L	E	S
E		T		E		E		E		E		S

HIDE AND SEEK

1. BONES. Simba likes to climB ON ESpecially high trees
2. MUSCLE. EMUS CLEarly are native to Australia, which has no indigenous cat breed.
3. TEETH. Cats can be mysterious and quiTE ETHereal by nature.
4. TEN. It is ofTEN said you don't choose a cat, it chooses you.
5. LIVES. The cats in the IsraeLI VESsel in the harbour were excellent mousers.

MULTIPLE CHEWS

1. **B.** Metro-Goldwyn-Mayer

2. **B.** Dinah

3. **D.** Patsy

4. **D.** Sergeant Tibbs

5. **C.** Persian

6. **C.** Duchess

7. **B.** Jake

8. **B.** Jonesy

9. **C.** Floyd

10. **D.** Michelle Pfeiffer

11. **B.** Jinx

12. **D.** Sassy

MYSTIC MOG

The four missing letters are F, H, I and S.

Rearranged they make the word FISH.

SIX FIX

1. Mouser, 2. Chases, 3. Adapts, 4. Patron, 5. Albino, 6. Bauble,
7. Jaguar, 8. Cajole, 9. Nicest, 10. Dental, 11. Sacred, 12. Tomcat.

CAT COLLAR

1. Kittens, 2. Stalked, 3. Disturb, 4. Bewitch, 5. Haddock.

CATWALK

TAGS

TOP LEFT: Bandages.

TOP RIGHT: Antiseptic.

LOWER CIRCLE: Gauze.

The letter in the centre common to all tags is an A.

KEEP IN SHAPE

MOGGY

GROOM

ANGORA

MARKING

THAT'S MY CAT

CHINCHILLA

CAT CODES

1. Skeleton, 2. Carefree, 3. Handsome, 4. Watchful, 5. Pedigree,
6. Snowshoe, 7. Mackerel, 8. Alleyway, 9. Hind legs, 10. Eyesight.

The proverb reads, 'When the cat's away the mice will play,'
meaning when the person in charge is absent, the workers
will not work quite as hard.

ALL THE SEVENS

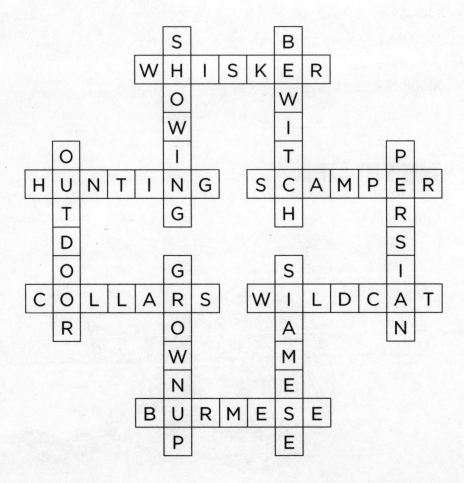

FORWARD

1. Fir, Fur, 2. Bails, Balls, 3. Morse, Mouse, 4. Torch, Touch.

TAKE A TUMBLE

1. Steer, Trees, Terse.

2. Acres, Races, Scare,

3. Palest, Staple, Plates.

GIVE ME FIVE!

B	R	E	E	D
O	■	N	■	A
W	A	T	E	R
L	■	E	■	T
S	O	R	T	S

MULTIPLE CHEWS

1. **B.** 'Runaway Boys'
2. **C.** Mississippi
3. **B.** Lightning Seeds
4. **D.** Orchestral Manoeuvres in the Dark
5. **C.** Tom Jones
6. **C.** Nicole Scherzinger
7. **D.** Yusuf Islam
8. **C.** Honky Cat
9. **D.** Ninety
10. **B.** Cradle
11. **C.** The Cure
12. **D.** Taylor Swift

STRAY CAT

Cactus

SEALPOINT

1. Near, 2. Errs, 3. Hair, 4. Used, 5. Free, 6. Mice.

NAME GAME

SNOWY is the cat that cannot be found.

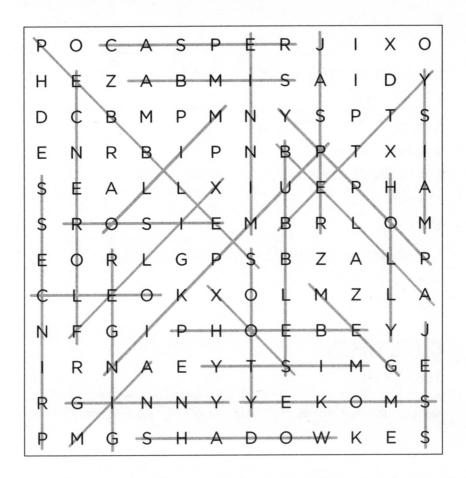

P O C A S P E R J I X O
H E Z A B M I S A I D Y
D C B M P M N Y S P T S
E N R B I P N B P T X I
S E A L L X I U E P H A
S R O S I E M B R L O M
E O R L G P S B Z A L R
C L E O K X O L M Z L A
N F G I P H O E B E Y J
I R N A E Y T S I M G E
R G I N N Y Y E K O M S
P M G S H A D O W K E S

LEAP TO IT!

TORTOISESHELL is the coded word.

1	2	3	4	5	6	7	8	9	10	11	12	13
L	E	A	P	G	V	B	C	Z	R	D	F	S

14	15	16	17	18	19	20	21	22	23	24	25	26
J	Y	N	H	T	X	I	M	O	U	Q	K	W

Words formed, reading from left to right and top to bottom of the grid:

ACROSS:
Litters, Terrain, Leap, Owner, Eats, Quiet, Sealpoint, Vet, Collars, Old, Parentage, Jumps, Lies, Munch, Manx, Malayan, Brushes.

DOWN:
Size, Stopped, Groom, Hear, Freedom, Kitten, Intelligent, Use, Lurk, Coat, Lap, Persian, Burmese, Animal, Charm, Meal, Need.

CLOCK WATCH

1. Eyesight (C), 2. Tracking (A), 3. Balances (C), 4. Activity (C), 5. Parasite (A), 6. Silently (A), 7. Harmless (C), 8. Resident (C).

FORWARD

1. Small, Smell, 2. Handy, Hardy, 3. Holes, Homes, 4. Hungers, Hunters.

STRAY CAT

Scattered

FELINE FIVES

1–2. Cameo, **3–4.** Meals, **5–6.** Black, **7–8.** Scent, **9–10.** Sneak, **11–12.** Nasal.

FITTING IN

1. Ate, **2.** Ran, **3.** Eye.

SPLITS

1. Rome, Siam,

2. Egypt, Japan,

3. Cyprus, Persia.

NINE LIVES

1. Ringing, **2.** Sharing, **3.** Shoals.

LONGHAIRS

MYSTIC MOG

The four missing letters are C, E, I and M.

Rearranged they make the word MICE.

SHADOW PLAY

1. Toy * Gum, 2. Cushion, 3. Descent, 4. Comfort, 5. Scratch,
6. Tangled, 7. Protect, 8. Leather, 9. Siamese, 10. Postman.

The expression is: 'The cat that got the cream.' This is how a situation may be described when a person (or a cat!) finds itself in a superior position and is rather smug about it.

SHADY SEVENS

1. Prowled, 2. Healthy, 3. Stroked, 4. Outside, 5. Agility,
6. Cat flap, 7. Sit down.

PERSIAN is formed in the shaded diagonal.

MULTIPLE CHEWS

1. **D.** Witch
2. **D.** T.S. Eliot
3. **B.** Judith Kerr
4. **C.** Hat
5. **A.** Beatrix Potter
6. **D.** Turkey
7. **C.** Slinky Malinki
8. **C.** Tennessee Williams
9. **D.** Winnie-the-Pooh
10. **A.** Crookshanks
11. **C.** Lion
12. **B.** Richard Parker

CAT COLLAR

1. Ragdoll, 2. Lapping, 3. Grown Up, 4. Pointed, 5. Deliver.

ALPHAGRAMS

1. Socks, Bill Clinton, 2. Mitsou, Marilyn Monroe,
3. Beelzebub, Mark Twain.

CRYPTI-CAT

S	■	S	■	S	L	E	E	P
P	E	T	S	■	I	■	A	■
E	■	R	■	S	T	A	R	T
L	E	A	P	■	T	■	S	■
L	■	W	A	T	E	R	■	S
■	K	■	R	■	R	O	O	M
M	E	W	E	D	■	V	■	A
■	E	■	N	■	D	E	A	R
S	P	O	T	S	■	R	■	T

TAGS

TOP LEFT: Duchess.

TOP RIGHT: Lucifer.

LOWER CIRCLE: Toulouse.

The letter in the centre common to all tags is a U.

SHADY SEVENS

1. Brushed, 2 Hunting, 3 Stretch, 4 Roaming, 5 Kittens, 6 Purpose, 7 Recline.

BURMESE is formed in the shaded diagonal.

OLD POSSUM

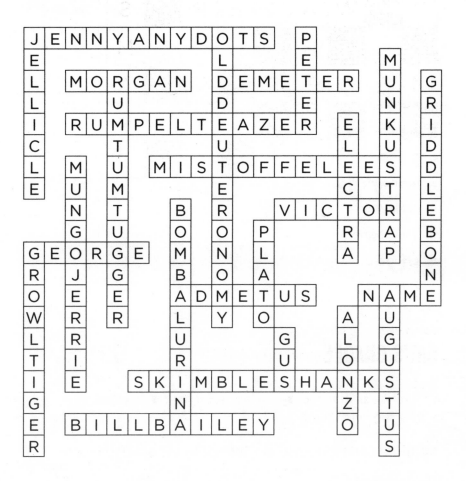

STRAY CAT

Activated

MULTIPLE CHEWS

1. **D.** Spike
2. **D.** Red
3. **B.** Benny the Ball
4. **C.** Japanese
5. **C.** Pink
6. **B.** Jess
7. **A.** Felix
8. **C.** Dog
9. **D.** Snowball
10. **B.** Mr Jinks
11. **C.** Lasagne
12. **C.** Figaro

CAT'S CRADLE

1. Slumber, 2. Snoozed, 3. Purring, 4. Evening, 5. Resides,
6. Running, 7. Mingled.

MORNING and EVENING are formed in the shaded crosses.

FELINE FIVES

1-2 Lilac, **3-4** Tamed, **5-6** Hears, **7-8** Brown, **9-10** Await, **11-12** Timid.

QUIZ CROSSWORD

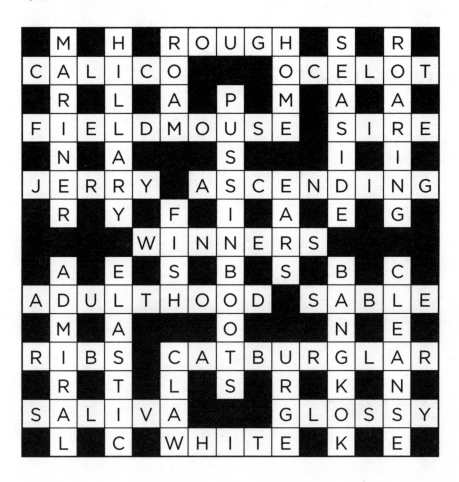

SIX FIX

1. Breeds, 2. Rattle, 3. Tunnel, 4. Tinned, 5. Cities, 6. Enters, 7. Reared,
8. Refuge, 9. Guided, 10. Demure, 11. Rubbed, 12. Debris.

ALL THE SEVENS

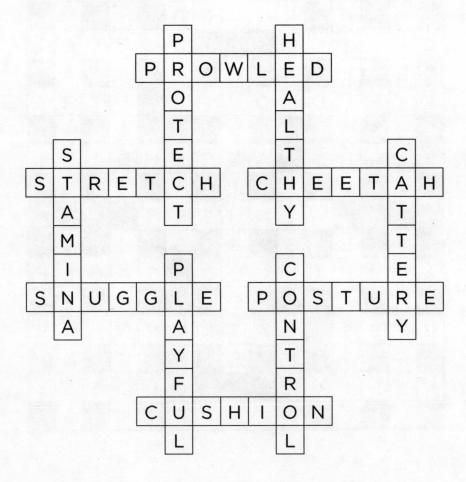

MYSTIC MOG

The four missing letters are O, S, T and Y.

Rearranged they make the word TOYS.

CAT COLLAR

1. Enjoyed, 2. Duchess, 3. Scamper, 4. Roobarb, 5. Bristle.

A TO Z

UNIQUE appears twice.

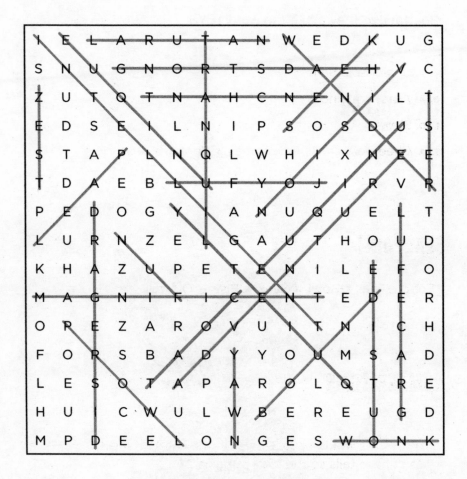

MULTIPLE CHEWS

1. **A.** Larry

2. **D.** Grumpy Cat

3. **B.** Karl Lagerfeld

4. **D.** Kindle

5. **C.** Fur

6. **A.** Baghdad

7. **A.** Alaska

8. **C.** 24

9. **A.** Unsinkable Sam

10. **A.** Abraham Lincoln

11. **D.** Stewie

12. **A.** Cheetah

SEALPOINT

1. Food, **2.** Idle, **3.** Bowl, **4.** Seek, **5.** Else, **6.** Owns.

NUMBER SUMS

A. 27.
Three cats would have 27 lives if one cat has nine. Lynxes don't have tails so the total remains 27.

B. 2024.
Cats was released in 2019 and a 'pride' is a group of lions, which has five letters.

C. Six.
Tom Kitten three letters, and the Owl another three letters.

CRYPTI-CAT

B		S		G	R	O	O	M
L	I	C	K		U		W	
A		A		A	M	E	N	D
C	A	N	S		P		S	
K		T	A	I	L	S		A
	B		C		E	A	T	S
D	A	I	R	Y		T		I
	T		E		B	A	N	D
S	H	A	D	E		N		E

TAGS

TOP LEFT: Demeter.

TOP RIGHT: Macavity.

LOWER CIRCLE: Electra.

The letter in the centre common to all tags is a T.

CAT BASKET

D	I	S	C
I	D	E	A
S	E	A	T
C	A	T	S

WHO AM I?

LARRY.

The first, third, fourth and fifth letters have no option available. The second letter could be an A or a C from the rhyme. A is the only option to combine with the letters given.

LARRY is the name of the brown-and-white tabby who moved into No. 10 Downing Street in 2011.

NUMBER NAMES

BARRY is worth 21. B = 1, O = 2, Y = 3, T = 4, A = 5, R = 6.

For BOB to be worth 4, the B has to be 1 and the O a 2 (1 + 2 + 1 = 4). BOBBY = 8. The values are 1 + 2 + 1 + 1 + Y. Y has to be 3. In TOBY the T is the only letter without a known value. T + 2 + 1 + 3 = 10. T has to be 4.

In TABBY the A is the only letter without a known value. 4 + A + 1 + 1 + 3 = 14. A must be 5. In BARRY the R is the only letter without a known value and 6 is the only digit to be placed. R = 6.

BARRY = 1 + 5 + 6 + 6 + 3 = 21.

KEEP IN SHAPE

PERSIAN

STRIPES

POSTURE

VARIETY

CAT CODES

1. Adopting, 2. Cheshire, 3. Devon Rex, 4. Luncheon, 5. Cinnamon, 6. Scavenge, 7. Tortoise, 8. Shelters, 9. Domestic, 10. Movement.

The proverb reads, 'A cat in gloves catches no mice' meaning an over-cautious approach achieves no result.

MULTIPLE CHEWS

1. **D.** Simba

2. **A.** Mr Bigglesworth

3. **B.** Black cat

4. **B.** Snowbell

5. **B.** *Meet the Parents*

6. **A.** Argus Filch

7. **C.** Mr Tinkles

8. **C.** Mike Myers

9. **A.** Antonio Banderas

10. **C.** Skunk

11. **D.** Mittens

12. **B.** Bob

CRYPTI-CAT

S	■	S	■	S	C	O	L	D
C	A	T	S	■	O	■	I	■
O	■	A	■	A	L	L	E	Y
R	I	F	T	■	O	■	S	■
E	■	F	E	M	U	R	■	S
■	G	■	N	■	R	O	L	L
G	U	I	D	E	■	C	■	I
■	M	■	O	■	S	K	I	N
U	S	I	N	G	■	S	■	K

FELINE FRIENDS

A – MAX – Cat 4 – Pandora – aged one.
B – KATIE – Cat 1– Tommy – aged five.
C – CELIA – Cat 2 – Peach – aged three.
D – MARCUS – Cat 3 – Jude – aged six.

NINE LIVES

1. Spanish, 2. Comic, 3. Chain.

CHAMPIONS

CLOCK WATCH

1. Ear drums (C), 2. Outdoors (C), 3. Identify (A), 4. Sourpuss (C), 5. Mistress (A), 6. Grooming (A), 7. Athletic (C), 8. Midnight (A).

GIVE ME FIVE!

T	I	G	E	R
A	■	R	■	I
L	O	O	K	S
O	■	O	■	K
N	A	M	E	S

FELINE FIVES

1-2. Moggy, 3-4. Agile, 5-6. Clean, 7-8. Yawns, 9-10. Enter,
11-12. Devon.

SHADOW PLAY

1. Whisker, 2. Habitat, 3. Plastic, 4. Musical, 5. Patient,
6. Sardine, 7. Dickens, 8. Abandon, 9. Forward, 10. Collars.

The question is: 'Was it a car or a cat I saw?' This is
a palindrome where the letters read the same forwards
and backwards.

FITTING IN

1. Vet, 2. Sit, 3. Fur.

STRAY CAT

Vacation

NOTES

NOTES

NOTES

NOTES

NOTES

NOTES

ALSO AVAILABLE

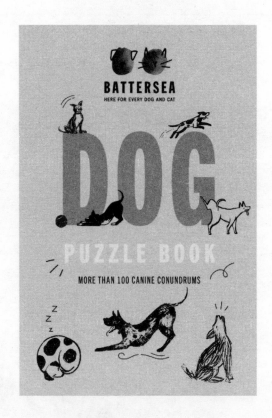

BATTERSEA DOG PUZZLE BOOK

ISBN 978 1 80279 412 0